£3

gen

17/48.

Stephen Crook's
CLASSIC STEAM
Collection

Silver Link Publishing

The Coach House, Garstang Road, St Michael's-on-Wyre, Lancashire, PR3 OTG.

CONTENTS

Front cover: 'Princess Royal' class 'Pacific' No. 46201 *Princess Elizabeth* makes a dramatic departure from Carlisle Citadel station with the 10am Euston-Perth in April 1962.

Previous page: 'A4' 4-6-2 No. 60010 *Dominion of Canada* approaches Hilton tunnel on the way out of Perth with the up 'Grampian' in August 1964. A grimy engine, when everything else seemed right for once, was rather disappointing!

Facing page: Drummond Class T9 'Greyhound' 4-4-0 No. 30120 approaches Tavistock North with the Up Plymouth portion of the 'Atlantic Coast Express' in May 1961. In those days, Tavistock had two stations, Tavistock South being for the Western Region. Now it is one of the many West Country towns that has no station at all, although the railway does still run to Gunnislake, a mere three miles or so away. No. 30120 is seen here with an authentic coat of BR grime: since 1962 the preserved engine has become the chameleon of the preservation scene. A National Collection engine, it has carried LSWR colours, BR lined black livery, and at the time of writing is painted in Southern Railway olive green, on the Mid Hants Railway.

Above: Midland 'Compound' 4-4-0 No. 41113 leaves Keighley with the 9.33am Morecambe-Leeds in November 1958. A fine sight indeed.

Copyright © Stephen Crook/Silver Link Publishing Ltd

Designed by Nigel Harris.   First published in the UK, November 1990

All rights reserved. No part of this publication may be reproduced, stored in a retrieval system, transmitted in any form, by any other means electronic or mechanical, or photocopied, or recorded by any other information storage and retrieval system, without prior permission in writing from the publisher.

Imagesetting by Ps&Qs, Liverpool and printed in the UK by The Amadeus Press, Huddersfield, Yorkshire.

British Library Cataloguing in Publication Data
Crook, Stephen
    Stephen Crook's classic steam collection.
    1. Railways, history
    I. Title
    385.09
    ISBN 0-947971-35-1

AUTHOR'S INTRODUCTION

Above: Saturday June 25 1960 is a rare cloudless day on Beattock as Kingmoor's 'Jubilee' 4-6-0 No 45724 *Warspite* makes a confident ascent of the bank with the relief to the down 'Royal Scot.' The smoke output at the front is being at least equalled by the LMS 2-6-4T banker, about to come into view. This location is often referred to as Harthope, this being the name of the only farm in the vicinity.

I f I have to admit that most of the pictures in this book are traditional in approach, then here too I shall follow the path of tradition and preface the contents with a few words of personal introduction.

Of the pictures that follow, the action shots cover roughly the last decade of BR steam, accompanied by a few views from earlier years. The pictures have been assembled fairly loosely on a geographical basis. Unlike the old timetables I have been perusing in recent weeks, I have started in the north, if only because that is the part of the country I have covered most widely. There was never any hope that I would be able to cover the country evenly; but it there are rather a high number of pictures from both North-West Scotland and North-West England, perhaps the fact that there are also a good number from East Anglia will provide some sort of balance. In any event, the pictures I have chosen are special favourites!

Although I actually took my first railway photograph in 1949, it was unfortunately not until 1957 that I started shooting moving trains, and it was not until the following year that I acquired a camera that was really suitable for the job. In the early 1950s, the disappointing results produced by my friends, who had photographed express trains with cameras whose fastest speed was one-hundredth of a second, had not inspired me to follow suit. Thus, for several years I remained content with 'still life' studies.

When I started photographing steam locomotives in

earnest, late in 1958, I decided to concentrate on older engines. This in itself, was probably one of the few things I did correctly, but I should not at the same time have almost completely ignored the more commonplace classes like 'Duchesses' in charge of the 'Royal Scot'! Of course, like all the best railway photographers of the time, I was only going to press the shutter when the sun was shining! This produced good results, but it also inevitably considerably restricted my output. It was not, as some people thought at the time, that my camera or technique were incapable of coping with dull weather; it was simply that the results looked so much better when the subject was bathed in sunshine.

So, for most of the period covered by this book I was always to some extent 'up against it.' It was rarely just a question of visiting the nearest railway line and photographing whatever might happen to come along. It was rather a matter of trying to guess which engines, or routes had the least life expectancy, finding the opportunity and then finding the means to visit the relevant areas. Also, it was crucial to listen carefully to the weather forecast before actually committing myself to a journey: money and resources were scarce and scrupulous planning was essential. Even so, if all this made railway photography more difficult, it also provided the greater incentive and the greater satisfaction when everything fell into place.

So what was my photographic philosophy? My principal aim was to obtain pictures which were as good a record as possible of these older engines at work; I decided that they they should be as sharp as possible, with a view to showing the greatest amount of detail. However, I was also concerned that the resulting photographs should be as pictorially pleasing as I could make them, and that they should be as flattering as possible to the locomotives depicted. A flattering portrayal of the subject is all-important in portrait photography and my attitude to trains is not very different. There are many different approaches to railway photography, but so far as I was concerned, with limited time and opportunity, and with older engine classes fast disappearing, the late 1950s was not a time to experiment with photography of a primarily pictorial nature. Each to his own!

If anyone is hoping to find pictures of enthusiasts excursions or preserved locomotives in this book, then I am

Below: An Edinburgh-Manchester train leaving Carlisle, at Wreay, in August 1960. In the summer months, the Glasgow-Manchester was due to leave Carlisle at 1.23pm, and this train was timed to leave at 1.47pm. Comprising mostly LMS stock, it included a through coach from Aberdeen and another from Dundee. The engine is 'Royal Scot' 4-6-0 No. 46104 *Scottish Borderer,* from Polmadie shed. The most apparent difference between the rebuilt 'Scot' and the rebuilt 'Patriot' from this angle was that the 'Scot' had a deeper bufferbeam. The two hours between mid-day and 2pm were always the busiest at Carlisle, particularly for southbound trains. But the two hours between midnight and 2am would have probably come to a close second!

Facing page: For many people, the GWR's branch lines were the epitome of the country railway: '45XX' class 2-6-2T No. 4574 is seen here near Sandplace Halt with the 10.35am (Sundays) train from Liskeard to Looe, in May 1961. This branch is nearly nine miles long, as the main line itself takes a more northerly course at this point. There was no intermediate place of any size en route, all four 'stations' being classed as halts.

Above: A westerly wind fortunately blows most of the leaking steam to the side as 'K2' 2-6-0 No. 61784 departs from Banavie with the 3.15pm from Fort William to Mallaig, in August 1960. The locomotive was in its last months: withdrawn in March 1961, the locomotive was reduced to scrap at Inverurie Works by the end of April.

afraid they will be disappointed. Preservation societies have done a remarkable job, but I have never had any urge to go out and photograph preserved trains. I regard the prospect with about as much enthusiasm as a big game hunter would relish a visit to the zoo. It is all too artificial, too commercialised and just too plain easy.

I cannot say I am very inspired by modern image BR power, but since 1968 I have been fortunate enough to make several very enjoyable trips abroad to photograph working steam. Unfortunately, even in the surviving far-flung outposts of ordinary steam working there are now an increasing number of specially-arranged trains, which makes the task of recording the everyday scene that much more difficult.

A few words about my photographic equipment might be of interest. My first camera was an *Ensign Selfix* 'two and a quarter by three and a quarter' which my father had used

before the war. The lens, an *Ensar Anastigmat,* gave good central definition, but this virtue was rather wasted as the camera had an vicious trigger and quite a lot of my early pictures showed at least some degree of camera shake. It had the dubious luxury of two view-finders, both of them being inadequate, in particular the minute eye-level one. The fastest speed was 1/100th of a second, but as I have indicated, I was not concerned with moving trains in those days. After a year or two I found that the best results were to be obtained by 'stopping down' to about f16, propping the camera on some handy firm support, and taking a time exposure.

In the mid-1950s, I tried two folding cameras with shutter speeds up to 1/250th of a second, with a view to photographing moving trains, but both these cameras had other faults. Finally, in 1958 I was assured by a friend that the best results would be obtained only with a plate camera. I therefore acquired an old *Goertz Anschutz* for about £20. This had a *Tessar* lens, which gave good results despite having a fair number of fine scratches on the surface. It had a focal-plane shutter, an essential requirement. This camera unfortunately was somewhat unreliable. The eye-level viewfinder was too small for comfort - for taking moving trains a viewfinder consisting of a large open wire frame on the lens panel would have been better. The camera was designed to take quarter-plate glass plates, which were still readily obtainable at the time.

After a certain amount of practice I obtained some reason-

Above: In 1952, I made a pilgrimage to Wick, in the school summer holidays, to see the last Highland Railway 4-4-0, *Ben Alder*. My modest pocket money of the day meant that it was only possible to make the journey by cycle, and by 'sleeping rough' at night. However, I allowed myself the dubious luxury of travelling by bus north from Inverness. From Dornoch to Wick, I reckoned the bus must have been nearly as old as *Ben Alder* ; it had wooden seats, my only such experience in Britain!

The journey was certainly worthwhile, particularly as No. 54398 slipped through the preservation net and was scrapped, despite remaining intact for several years. I saw the engine as late as 1957, in the small shed at Boat of Garten. No. 54398 is standing at Wick, in August 1952. Built in 1898 by Drummond, the 4-4-0 was later fitted with a Caledonian Railway boiler, as were all the members of the class that survived the war.

able pictures, but after the shutter failed the following year I brought a *Super Ikonta* as a reserve camera. This I used most of the time in 1959 and 1960. I reverted to the plate camera in 1961, after the shutter had been repaired for a second time. This camera I then used regularly until June 1968, when the shutter collapsed completely – probably in sympathy with the imminent demise of BR steam!

Whilst I am quite happy to be known as a 'railway photographer', it is really the 'railway' half of that term which is dominant. The 'photography' part is primarily a means to an end. However, I have certainly developed and printed myself all the photographs that appear in this book, and also derived pleasure from this activity – although it has involved the occasional love-hate relationship in the darkroom with a difficult negative. Printing is one of those activities that can be immensely satisfying when you think you have made just the right print, but extremely frustrating when you cannot get it quite right.

In 1964 I had realised that if I was even going to start taking colour slides the moment should not be delayed as the red 'Duchesses' might not survive much longer. I managed to obtain a *Zeiss Contaflex* on semi-permanent loan from my brother, with which I fired away at some of the more obvious subjects. It was actually a disappointing camera, certainly by modern standards, and despite its *Tessar* lens, the definition declined noticeably at the edges. Anyway, it was very much a second string to my black and white work, the best of which appears in this book.

Although most of my railway photography today is in colour, I have no regrets about concentrating on black and white photography in the last decade of BR steam. Apart from the limitations of colour in the early 1960s, the medium of black and white somehow seemed right for the era. It is good to know that some of the best railway photographers today still prefer monochrome.

A summary of my equipment would not be complete without a mention of my faithful transport machines. Pride of place must go to my *Super Lenton* bicycle, built by Raleigh in 1955, which is still going strong in my possession, after the mechanised vehicles have been passed on to

others. Most of the photographic locations in the Carlisle area were reached with its assistance, and after 33 years on the road it certainly owes me nothing. In 1959, I acquired (cheaply) a 150cc BSA *Bantam* motorcycle to enable me to travel slightly longer distances, but then one day the following year (whilst I was away from home) my mother sold it to the window cleaner - probably with a view to increasing my life expectancy! I pretended to be most put-out, but was secretly rather pleased as this gave me a stronger claim to the use of the old family car. This was a 1937 *Austin 10 Conway Cabriolet*, a most reliable car which I believe still exists today. Although the interior was not the last word in luxury, it had the invaluable facility of allowing the passenger's front seat to be removed, thus enabling me to sleep in the car; in this way it saved me quite a lot of money and made it possible for me to be on location at sunrise should the occasion arise. Even when, in 1964, I acquired a much faster car (largely to enable me to pursue trains more successfully) the old car was still usually the preferred choice for an overnight job. Nowadays, unfortunately, if I want to find some proper steam, I have to travel by aeroplane. How times change.

In conclusion, I would like to thank the staff at the Morton Community Centre, here in Carlisle for allowing me to use the darkroom facilities and for all their friendly assistance. I should like also to thank Robert Leslie for reminding me of some times and places that I had long since forgotten. Finally I should like to express my gratitude to Nigel and Jayne Harris, of SLP, for all their help with this book.

Stephen Crook,
Carlisle,
Cumbria,

September 1990.

STEPHEN CROOK'S CLASSIC STEAM COLLECTION

NORTH OF INVERNESS

Above: In 1959, the Inverness-Tain 'locals' were still worked exclusively by splendid Pickersgill 4-4-0s, usually in very respectable external condition. Here, No 54470 skirts the Cromarty Firth, just west of Invergordon, with the 3.45pm from Tain in September 1959. My main consideration in selecting this precise location was that the angle of the sun was not too 'frontal' – over most of this section the train would have been heading straight into the sun.

Left: The 3.18pm from Inverness to Tain leaves Alness behind CR 4-4-0s Nos. 54496 and 54493, in September 1959. No. 54496 was working her passage back to Wick, after receiving attention at Inverness. This engine was the only one of the class that I noted without the normal BR lining.

Right: CR 0-4-4 T No. 55199 runs into Alness with a local freight from Inverness in September 1959; latterly this was the only member of the class to be shedded at Inverness, and this seemed to be the locomotive's regular working. In other areas, this class would have been associated with local passenger or banking duties. In keeping with the best tradition of Inverness shed, 55199 was usually very clean, possibly to the detriment of the paintwork, which was worn down to bare metal on parts of the splashers.

Above: A last look at the Inverness-Tain 'locals' a few weeks before the service was withdrawn, at the start of the summer timetable. In April 1960, 4-4-0 No. 54488 hurries away from Conon (which serves Conon Bridge) with the 9.45am from Tain. This engine carries a 60B (Aviemore) shedplate and would not normally be seen north of Inverness. It would more usually have been employed assisting trains from Aviemore to Slochd Summit.

STEPHEN CROOK'S CLASSIC STEAM COLLECTION

Above: CR 4-4-0 No. 54487 and a Stanier Class 5 4-6-0 are climbing away from Garve on the line to Kyle of Lochalsh on a humid day in September 1959. The train is the 10.30am from Inverness; this took a pilot between Dingwall and Achanalt summit (ten miles west of Garve) if required; thus the train was piloted in the summer months. No. 54487 was the regular engine for this job, being sub-shedded at Dingwall for this purpose.

Above: Class 5 4-6-0 No. 44959 drifts down from Achanalt past lonely Loch Culen with a Kyle of Lochalsh-Inverness freight in September 1959. The mountain on the left is Fionn Bheinn. The telegraph poles look as though they have been rough-hewn from a nearby forest!

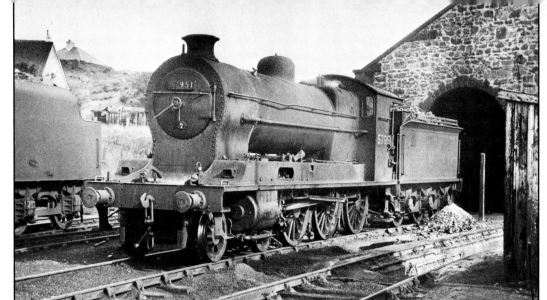

Right: Highland Railway 'Clan Goods' 4-6-0 No. 57951 stands outside the shed at Kyle of Lochalsh, in August 1950. Designed by Cumming in 1918, these were the only HR 4-6-0s to survive until the mid-1950s. Despite their name, they could be seen also on passenger trains in their later years.

Above: HR 0-4-4T No. 55051 is the subject of the fitters' attentions inside Inverness shed, in 1953. Designed by Drummond in 1905, this locomotive was retained (together with sister engine 55053) for working the branch from Dornoch to the Mound, in Sutherland. After the withdrawal of No. 55053 in 1957, the line was worked by GWR 0-6-0PTs Nos. 1646 and 1649. The branch finally closed in June 1960. By 1953, most engines would have received the new BR emblem, in preference to the full lettering shown here. Slightly less old, my faithful *Hercules* can be seen leaning against the shed wall. My saddlebag must have been at the local Youth Hostel!

Right: LMS 'Jinty' 0-6-0T No. 47541 stands outside the distinctive open roundhouse at Inverness, in August 1950. The livery is a typical hybrid of the era - the early style of BR renumbering on the bunker with LMS lettering still on the tankside, and, in this instance, no front number plate at all!

THE WEST HIGHLAND LINE

Left: Three West Highland stalwarts at Fort William shed in August 1950. Gresley's newer 'Mogul' for the line, the 'K4,' introduced in 1937, is flanked by two of his earlier 'K2s', dating from 1914. The precise designation was 'K2/2,' indicating that the engine had been fitted with side-window cabs, a very desirable refinement for those locomotives which had been transferred to the West Highland line. Several also received the names of lochs situated near to the line. From the left the engines are: 'K2/2' No 61791 *Loch Laggan*, 'K4' No. 61998 *Macleod of Macleod*, and 'K2/2' *Loch Oich*.

Above: In the early 1960s, most of the signals on the West Highland line were still of the fine North British lower quadrant semaphore variety, with distinctive pear-shaped spectacle glasses. These signals had no ladders, the lamp being raised and lowered by a winch. Here, a well-preserved example gives a clear road from Banavie to 'K1' 2-6-0 No. 62011 with the 1.5pm from Mallaig in August 1960; this was the last station before Fort William. In 1960, the 'K1' 2-6-0s were in charge of most of the trains on the Mallaig extension, despite the arrival of a BR Standard 'Mogul' during the summer. Although 'B1' 4-6-0s, BR 4-6-0s and LMS Class 5MT 4-6-0s were regularly used between Glasgow and Fort William, the smaller and lighter 'K1s' were preferred on the extension to Mallaig.

Below: 'K2' 2-6-0 No. 61784 climbs to Glenfinnan station with the 10.40am Fort William-Mallaig goods, during April 1960. The six-wheeled fish wagons are an interesting reminder that if it had not been for the anticipated fish trade the extension to Mallaig would probably never have been built. It is ironic that although the line survives, the fish brought ashore at Mallaig now travels by road. When this train first came into view a mile or so away across the other side of the glen, there seemed no prospect whatsoever of the sun shining at the crucial moment. However, when the train reached me five minutes later a fortuitous hole had appeared in the clouds – to be followed a few minutes later by a lengthy hailstorm! Such is the speed at which the weather can change in the West Highlands.

Right: The braes of Lochaber stretch out behind the train as BR 'Standard' 4-6-0 No 73078 and a 'B1' 4-6-0 head south near Tulloch with the 3.5pm departure from Fort William to Glasgow, during August 1960. The 11 coaches comprise an interesting assortment of Gresley and BR stock, the seventh coach being still in the photogenic cream and vermilion livery dating from the mid-1950s. The last vehicle (on the centre of the bridge) is an observation car.

STEPHEN CROOK'S CLASSIC STEAM COLLECTION

Below: 'K1' 2-6-0 No 62012 between Lochailort and Arisaig with the 3.15 pm Fort William-Mallaig service, in September 1959. This train (including a through coach from Glasgow) was one of several trains on this line that ran during the summer months only. The fine NBR distant signal still carries the old type of lamp, distinguishable by its ornate top. Upper quadrant semaphore signals survived on this route until 1988.

Left: Later on the same day, No 62012 is returning to Fort William with the 5.40pm 'mixed' from Mallaig. The 2-6-0 is seen hurrying along near Morar as the evening shadows lengthen. Another passenger train left Mallaig for Fort William at 6.25 pm. It was surprising that even during the summer months two similar trains should run within an hour of each other; however, the 6.25pm departure would be timed to connect with the 6.00pm arrival of the boat from Armadale, on Skye, and might therefore be subject to delay.

Right: Class 5MT 4-6-0 No. 45159 and a BR 'Standard' 4-6-0 climb through Glen Lochy with the 9.30am Oban-Glasgow train in August 1961. The long and steep ascent between Dalmally and Tyndrum makes this the most difficult section on the eastbound journey; not surprisingly, this train was normally double-headed during the summer. Unlike the line from Fort William, the railway is never very far from the road between Oban and Crianlarich. This line had been finally completed in 1880, the first section from Dunblane having been started 22 years earlier. The eastern half of the line, between Crianlarich Lower and Dunblane, was closed in 1965.

Above: At the southern end of the West Highland line, Class 'C15' 4-4-2T No. 67474 approaches Glen Douglas and the summit of the climb from Arrochar with the 1.5pm (Saturdays Only) train to Craigendoran in March 1959. The outline of the engine is slightly marred by the extra fittings required for the push-pull operation. Like all passenger trains on the West Highland, the train is carrying express headlamps! These engines worked the service for only a few more months, after which a 'J37' 0-6-0 was in charge for a few weeks before a diesel railbus took over. By 1964, this local service had been withdrawn. No. 67474 was built by the Yorkshire Engine Company in 1913 as NBR Class M. Together with sister engine 67460 it was withdrawn in April 1960, the last pair of survivors.

16

EAST SCOTLAND

Below: The last Great North of Scotland Railway 'D40' 4-4-0, No. 62277 *Gordon Highlander* performs its last duties under BR ownership as station pilot at Kittybrewster in April 1958. I had gone to Aberdeen especially to see it and was relieved to find that it was still in steam. This engine had the dubious distinction for several years of having the same name as another BR locomotive - LMS 'Scot' No. 46106. The success of these locomotives might be judged by the fact that this engine was built as late as 1921 to a design first introduced in 1899. After withdrawal it was quickly preserved (perhaps too quickly, for initially it was painted in the wrong shade of green) and by 1959 it was working excursion trains.

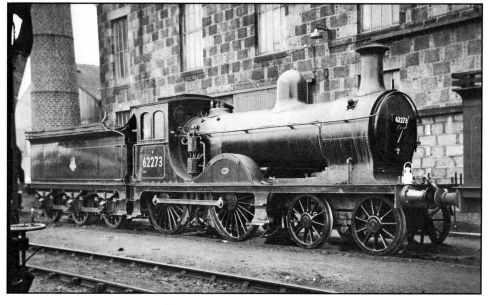

Left: Class D40 4-4-0 No 62273 *George Davidson* stands outside Inverurie Works in 1953 after a complete overhaul. Inverurie was 16 miles north-west of Aberdeen on the line to Inverness, and in addition to GNSR locomotives, the works repaired NBR engines from all parts of Scotland.

Above: By 1966, the Aberdeen-Glasgow services provided the last opportunity north of London to see 'Pacifics' regularly at work on express trains. Here 'A4' No. 60024 *Kingfisher* darts under one of the bridges just south of Stonehaven in August 1966 with the up 'Grampian', which left Aberdeen at 1.30pm. Although a named train, this was not one of the famous three-hour expresses: stopping at nearly every station, this train took exactly four hours for the journey. The diamond-shaped plaque depicting a Kingfisher, which this engine carried latterly on the left-side only, can be seen above the centre driving wheel.

Right: NBR Class J37 0-6-0 No. 64611 is seen between Bridge of Dun and Brechin with the daily freight from Montrose. The central portion of this journey entailed running over the Aberdeen-Perth main line for about three miles. This picture was taken on March 30 1967, the penultimate day of steam working on the branch.

STEPHEN CROOK'S CLASSIC STEAM COLLECTION

Top: Gresley 'V2' 2-6-2 No. 60919 comes off the Tay Bridge at Wormit, in charge of the 9.10 am (SO) Dundee-Blackpool, in August 1966. This was very much a 'height of the season' train, and in 1966 it ran only from June 25 to August 20. Arrival time at Blackpool North was 4.58pm. The 'V2' would unfortunately be detached at Edinburgh, the journey over the Waverley route being by diesel. The lines on the right of the picture are for the Tayport branch. The wind direction had forced me to take the photograph from the shady side of the track, and I think the result shows that on the other side the smoke would have obscured most of the train. The gentleman leaning out of the first coach with his camera also seems to favour this side!

Above: Deliberations appear to be holding up the departure from Dundee of the 10.10am goods to Carnoustie, in April 1967. The crew seems ready for the rightaway. 'B1' 4-6-0 No. 61102 may be unique in having an inverted shedcode - the plate reads 'B62' instead of '62B!'

Top: The cliffs above Dundee esplanade provide an adequate shelter from the strong northerly wind as 'B1' 4-6-0 No 61354 makes a smoky departure with the 2.50pm goods for Perth, during April 1967. By this time, this should have been a diesel working – but I was lucky on this occasion!

Above: With the Sidlaw Hills in the background, Gresley 'V2' 2-6-2 No. 60813 nips smartly along near Glencarse in August 1966, with the early morning Dundee-Perth empty stock train. Although barely apparent here, this engine was unique in being fitted with a stove-pipe chimney and small smoke deflectors on top of the smokebox - so that what it lost in looks it gained in interest. Together with sister engine No. 60919, it was latterly kept in fine external condition at Dundee shed.

Above: Kinnoull Hill provides an impressive background as 'A2' class 'Pacific' No 60530 *Sayajirao* approaches Perth with the morning ECS train from Dundee in August 1966. This Peppercorn 'A2' was built at Doncaster in 1948 and withdrawn in November 1966.

Left: Numerically, the last of the 'A4s,' No. 60034 *Lord Faringdon* passes Hilton Junction, about three miles south of Perth, with the up 'Grampian' in August 1965. Without wishing any disrespect to the human sources of 'A4' names, it is a fact that the nameplates featuring the original bird names are now appreciably more valuable. In this instance the peregrine was ousted! The tracks diverging to the right were part of the old route to Edinburgh, via Glenfarg. This was by far the most direct route but was closed because it served few important intermediate towns. Hilton Junction was understandably a popular photographic spot, providing an interesting and well-balanced location.

Above: Hilton Junction from the opposite direction to that shown on page 21, and illustrating the important signal box. Rebuilt 'Patriot' 4-6-0 No. 45535 *Sir Herbert Walker KCB* is passing with a down freight in August 1963. Engines from Carlisle (Kingmoor) regularly came to Perth both on passenger and freight workings.

Above: A very pleasant surprise one day in October 1958 was this sighting of the royal train, heading south out of Perth station, hauled by two gleaming Class 5MT 4-6-0s, Nos. 44704 and 44721. I did not have the opportunity to try and discover exactly who was on the train - it could presumably have been the Queen, returning to London after her autumn visit to Balmoral.

STEPHEN CROOK'S CLASSIC STEAM COLLECTION

Top: In the early 1960s, there were still several Caledonian signals to be seen around Perth. With the station still just visible on the left, 'V2' 2-6-2 No 60970 passes a bracket of lower quadrant semaphores with an Edinburgh train in April 1960. No. 60970 was one of the 'V2s' which latterly acquired outside steam pipes. 'V2s' did not regularly feature in the Perth allocation, but this engine is carrying a 63A (Perth) shedplate.

Above: By 1963, all the semaphores around Perth station had been replaced by colour light signals. In this picture, 'V2' 2-6-2 No. 60919, recently ex-works, is seen leaving with the Up 'postal' during August 1963. It was pleasing to find the impressive LMS-style livery on the mail coaches still in evidence at this time.

Right: Stanier Class 5MT 4-6-0 No. 44997 emerges from the cutting south of Gleneagles with the 3.30pm Aberdeen-Glasgow in August 1966. The bridge carries the A823 Crieff-Dunfermline road.

Below: 'A4' No. 60007 *Sir Nigel Gresley* with the down 'St Mungo.' The train is approaching Dunblane in May 1965. This three-hour train left Glasgow (Buchanan Street) at 5.30pm and was due to arrive at Aberdeen at 8.30pm. I recall that the balmy evening was slightly spoiled by a hidden danger concealed in the cow parsley - whilst waiting for this train I trod on a rusty nail which went straight through the sole of my shoe and into my foot!

For several decades, the NBR 4-4-0s had charge of many of the local trains in Fife, but when this picture was taken in April 1959, their reign was nearly over. Fife was moreover the last area where these engines could regularly be seen at work. Here, 'D30' 'Scott' 4-4-0 No. 62436 *Lord Glenvarloch* is seen at Inverkeithing with the 3.47pm to Thornton Junction, via Dunfermline. Despite being in an apparently healthy condition, the engine was in fact

withdrawn two months later. These engines were distinguishable from the 'D34' 'Glen' 4-4-0s in having larger driving wheels – 6ft 6in as opposed to 6ft. The rounded shape of the later LNER coaches shown here gives them an appearance reminiscent of LMS designs, but the bogie frames confirm their origin.

Above: 'V2' 2-6-2 No. 60813, the only example to be fitted with stovepipe chimney and small smoke deflectors, climbs from Inverkeithing to the Forth Bridge with the 9.10am(SO) Dundee-Blackpool service, during August 1966.

Right: A clean 'D11/2' 4-4-0, No. 62677 *Edie Ochiltree* pulls away from St Monance with the 12.48pm from Crail to Thornton Junction, in October 1958. Although not the last of the class to be withdrawn, it was the last to see active service. The class only became officially extinct after the withdrawal of No. 62678 *Luckie Mucklebackit*, but that engine spent its last year as a stationary boiler at Slateford Laundry, in Edinburgh. These engines were built by Gresley in 1924 for use in Scotland and were very similar to Robinson's 'Improved Director' design for the Great Central Railway. The main visible difference was the less shapely chimney, required in order to bring the 4-4-0s within the NBR loading gauge. Though they were still known as 'Directors' the name was less relevant to the Scottish version as none carried names of company directors. Instead, the authorities continued the practice, commenced with the 'D29' class 'Scott' engines, of using the splendid names of characters in the 'Waverley' novels.

STEPHEN CROOK'S CLASSIC STEAM COLLECTION

Left: 'D34' 'Glen' 4-4-0 No 62478 *Glen Quoich* potters along near Pittenweem with the 7.32am through train from Dundee to Glasgow in October 1958. In 1945, one 'D29' , one 'D30' and one 'D34' had been experimentally fitted with a 6.5in extension to the smokebox, the official reason being an attempt to prevent burning of the smokebox door. No. 62478 was the 'D34' thus modified and retained this feature until withdrawal in December 1959.

Above: April showers are brewing as 'D34' 4-4-0 No. 62478 *Glen Quoich* heads east between Thornton Junction and Cameron Bridge with a morning train on the Fife Coast line in April 1959. The first two coaches are still in the colourful cream and vermilion livery – most British stock had by this time been repainted in maroon, a less rewarding livery for black and white photographers. East of Leven, the line was single track. A considerable variety of trains used it and some went to Crail, a few only to Anstruther; some went to Dundee, others only as far as Leuchars Junction. In 1959, I did not usually bother to photograph trains with a mere 'B1' on the front!

Above: A strong west wind blows the dense smoke out to sea as snowplough-fitted 'J36' 0-6-0 No. 65345 struggles up from Seafield Colliery, with a load of coal, in February 1967. This pit was situated between Kirkcaldy and Kinghorn, and is now closed. No. 65345 was nearly 80 years old when this picture was taken, and was one of the last of the class to survive.

Right: 'J38' 0-6-0 No. 65921 passes Benarty Hill, near Kelty, with a short freight from Thornton Junction to Milnathort, in September 1966. The 'J38s' were similar in appearance to the more numerous 'J39s' (which had all been withdrawn by 1963) but were distinguishable by their lack of splashers, as a result of their having smaller wheels. This was one of the rare occasions when the sun was shining not on me, but actually on the train!

STEPHEN CROOK'S CLASSIC STEAM COLLECTION

Above: 'J37' 0-6-0 No. 64574 and 'K2' 2-6-0 No 61788 *Loch Rannoch* return to base at Eastfield after a day's shunting in the Linlithgow area, in April 1961. This picture was taken near Castlecary. After their withdrawal from the West Highland line, a few 'K2s' lingered briefly at Eastfield and were employed mainly on local freight workings, but they had all been condemned before the end of 1961.

Above: After the electrics came – and went! Many of Glasgow's suburban services had been electrified on November 7 1960. However the new 25kV ac units were found to be defective, and were all temporarily withdrawn after six weeks at work. The speed and efficiency with which the resulting complex reorganisation was carried out is recorded as one of BR's finer moments. In this picture, 'V1' 2-6-2T No. 67680 is approaching Milngavie in April 1961, with an evening suburban train from Queen Street. The wire at the left of the smokebox is part of the cable equipment used for releasing the coupling automatically when banking on Cowlairs bank.

Right: The name and worksplate of 'D34' 4-4-0 No. 62498 *Glen Moidart*, inside Eastfield shed in 1952. The 'Scotts', 'Glens', and Scottish 'Directors' did not have brass nameplates - names were simply painted onto the splashers. Despite the date, the name of this engine is still in the splendid LNER style, with white outline and red shading. Normally, the name was positioned exactly half-way down the splasher, so this example has a slightly unusual appearance. This picture shows to good advantage the splasher extension, to which the worksplate was bolted, and how it was neatly shaped to accommodate the coupling rod at the top of its revolution. The number on the worksplate still reads 2498, and it was destined to stay like that until the engine was withdrawn. Unlike the Works at Inverurie and Darlington Cowlairs rather sensibly decided that it was unnecessary to add '6' to the LNER number or otherwise tamper with it. After all, every LNER engine had been renumbered in 1946, and to have to change the workplates twice within a decade was a bit much!

Above: Even in steam days, Parkhead was probably better known as the home of Celtic Football Club than for its motive power depot. It had a fairly large allocation, although this consisted mostly of suburban passenger and freight locomotives. The engines on display here are mainly 'V1' and 'V3' 2-6-2Ts, 'N15' 0-6-2Ts, and 'K2' 2-6-0s. Despite the fact that it is April 1952, the nearest 'K2,' No 61772 *Loch Lochy*, is still carrying LNER green livery. The picture serves as a reminder of those Sunday afternoons when you could peer over an engine shed wall, or bridge parapet and see lines of slumbering engines awaiting the start of the next working week.....

STEPHEN CROOK'S CLASSIC STEAM COLLECTION

Left: St. Margarets shed, at Edinburgh, had a much larger allocation of engines than could ever be accommodated at any one time, with the result that on Sundays locomotives were regularly stabled in nearby sidings, alongside the main line. Small tank engines, however, were in a somewhat privileged position, having their own accommodation reserved in a private little roundhouse (albeit uncovered) on the opposite side of the main line. In August 1950, one of the occupants was still unrenumbered 'Y9' 0-4-0ST No. 8098. These engines were unpretentiously classified as '0F.'

Above: One of the handsome 'D20' 4-4-0s at Tweedmouth shed in August 1951. Originally designed by Worsdell in 1899, No. 62375 was one of only four members of the class rebuilt with long-travel valves in 1936 and officially classified 'D20/2.' They were regarded as a very successful engine, and outlasted most other 4-4-0s of similar vintage. Their last regular workings were 30 miles down the coast on the Alnmouth-Alnwick branch, but by the end of 1957 their active life was over.

Left: At the east end of Haymarket Works in August 1950,'J88' 0-6-0T No. 8328 is 'brewing up' for action. This engine was evidently the works 'pet' and always kept in very clean external condition. But even more important in my eyes and probably the main reason for the photograph was that this was one of the few engines that still had LNER letters and numbers two and a half years after Nationalisation. I always felt that this shed should have been known as Murrayfield; it was nearly a mile from Haymarket station, but overlooked the rugby ground.

BEATTOCK & THE GSWR

Above: 'Princess Coronation' class 'Pacific' No 46256 *Sir William Stanier FRS* makes an effortless accent of Beattock with the down 'Royal Scot' on June 25 1960. The train is approaching Greskine signalbox, about half-way up the bank. This engine, built under Ivatt but named after the original designer of the class, was one of only two which represented the ultimate mechanical development of this class. By the time of their construction, however (1947) appearance was being sacrificed for expediency; not only had the framework behind the cylinders been cut away, but also the bottom of the cab sidesheets had been pruned to allow for greater accessibility of the working parts.

Right: One of the most interesting workings in South Scotland in the early 1950s was the use of a Webb LNWR 2-4-2T to work the two-miles branch from Beattock to Moffat. Why this was thought necessary is not apparent, as the push-pull service was quite happily worked by one of the ubiquitous 'Caley' 0-4-4Ts, after this engine's withdrawal. The passenger service was discontinued in 1954, although the line remained open for freight. In this picture, No. 46656 is nearly ready to depart from the bay platform at Beattock with a midday train in August 1950.

For once, the sun comes out instead of just 'going in' as Stanier 'Princess Royal' class 'Pacific' No. 46203 *Princess Margaret Rose* climbs Beattock with the 10am Euston-Perth on August 18 1962. The heavy train of 13 coaches is being banked a Class 4MT 2-6-4T. The best news at Easter 1962 had been the surprise return to service of the 'Princess Royals' after they had been put into store the previous winter. Nos. 46200, 46201 and 46203 were transferred to Kingmoor motive power depot, where, along with the 'Duchesses,' they were regularly employed on the Perth turns. The hills in the background in this classic Beattock scene have now inevitably been affected by the creeping afforestation which has detracted from much of the lowland scene in recent years.

Top: BR 'Standard' 2-6-4T No. 80117 crosses the viaduct over the River Urr, west of Dalbeattie with the 6pm local train from Dumfries to Kirk-cudbright on June 9 1965, during the final week of operation. The Kirk-cudbright branch diverged from the main line at Castle Douglas, where there was a connection for Stranraer. From the start of the summer timetable that year, the Dumfries-Stranraer section closed. Surprisingly, in 1990, a few through trains still run from Euston to Stranraer via Kil-marnock, a detour of about 70 miles compared with the old journey.

Above: The return working for the 'Thames Clyde' express pilot was the 3.8pm 'stopper' from Dumfries to Glasgow St Enoch. On September 4 1959, '2P' 4-4-0 No. 40645 is seen about two miles north of Dumfries on the more leisurely northbound journey. This train will take 2hr 24min for the 82 miles to Glasgow. The original chimney on the engine, the GSWR semaphore route indicator positioned just above the bufferbeam, and the ageing non-corridor LMS coach all help to give a period atmosphere to the scene.

STEPHEN CROOK'S CLASSIC STEAM COLLECTION

THE WAVERLEY ROUTE

Above: The fireman casts a wary glance in my direction as his 'V2' 2-6-2, No. 60810, storms up through the woods between Penton and Kershopefoot with the 11.15am Carlisle-Millerhill freight, during September 1964. After looking at the ordnance survey map, I had earmarked this place as being the one spot south of Riccarton where the sun would still be on the front of the train. Needless to say, it was also the place where the train was furthest from any road and therefore involved the longest walk to the trackside!

Left: The Christmas trees of Kershopefoot line the track as the 2.15pm Carlisle-Millerhill freight passes behind Gresley 'V2' 2-6-2 No. 60824 in April 1964. This was one of the 'V2s' latterly fitted with outside steam pipes. Although this railway ran close to the Anglo-Scottish border for several miles, it was not until Kershopefoot that the line finally crossed into Scotland.

Below: Thompson 'B1' 4-6-0 No. 61244 *Strang Steel* waits impatiently to depart from Riccarton with the 2.15pm Carlisle-Millerhill freight in August 1964. This 'junction in the middle of nowhere' came into being as the point where the Border Countries line from Hexham joined the Waverley route. It ceased however to be a junction after 1956, when the line from Hexham was closed. When I revisited Riccarton in more recent times, after 23 years, I was very surprised to find considerable activity; the whole site was being excavated, and lorries were taking away loads of ash – apparently for use in power stations!

STEPHEN CROOK'S CLASSIC STEAM COLLECTION

Above: Gresley 'A3' class 'Pacific' No. 60097 *Humorist* coasts down the hill between Riccarton and Steele Road with the 5.22pm from Edinburgh to Carlisle in August 1960. It was the only one of the class to be fitted with conventional smoke deflectors – an appropriate choice perhaps, for as early as 1931, *Humorist* had been one of two 'A3s' chosen for various smoke deflection experiments. It was also the first 'A3' to be fitted with a double chimney. The deflectors were retained until the locomotive was withdrawn in August 1963.

Above: Class 'A2/3' 4-6-2 No. 60512 *Steady Aim* leaves Carlisle with the 4.15pm freight to Millerhill, in April 1964. This particular variety of 'A2' was built in 1946. The train is seen just after the point where the Waverley route, having taken a wide sweep to the west, crossed the West Coast Main Line near Kingmoor on a motorway-style flyover.

Above: One of the saddest spectacles of the later steam years was the sight of express locomotives on humble freight duties. Gresley 'A4' class 'Pacific' No. 60024 *Kingfisher* passes Parkhouse, just north of Carlisle, with the 4.15pm freight to Millerhill, in August 1963. When this picture was taken, the modest bridge at the right carried the A74, the main Carlisle-Glasgow road. Just at the far side of the bridge was Parkhouse Halt, a private station for the hearby RAF Maintenance Unit. Shortly after this, No. 60024 was transferred to Aberdeen, where she regained some of her former glory on the expresses to Glasgow.

Above: By the summer of 1961, many of the Carlisle-Hawick local services were in the hands of BR 'Standard' locomotives. Here, Riddles '2MT' class 2-6-0 No. 78046 is climbing to Shankend with the 12.25pm(SO) Hawick-Carlisle 'stopper' on August 12 1961. The balancing SO working back from Carlisle left at 9.19pm – well before closing time!

STEPHEN CROOK'S CLASSIC STEAM COLLECTION

Left: Thompson 'B1' 4-6-0 No. 61349 has charge of the 6.13pm service to Hawick in April 1964. The train is climbing the incline which took the Waverley route over the LMS Anglo-Scottish main line, at Kingmoor. The line in the foreground was a spur built in connection with the new Kingmoor marshalling yard.

Above: Passing Carlisle No. 3 signalbox is Class D49/2 'Hunt' 4-4-0 No 62744 *The Holderness,* arriving with the 6.30am 'stopping' train from Hawick in April 1960. Although most of the 'D49/1' 'Shire' class engines were based in Scotland, this was one of only two 'Hunts' that strayed north of the border. Hawick shed provided engines for the Hawick-

Carlisle 'locals', so, although 62744 has no shedplate, she would at this time either be a Hawick engine, or possibly on loan from St. Margarets. The engine was a fairly regular performer on this train in 1960, thus returning to her former haunts, for as a Gateshead engine in the 1940s, No. 62744 could often be seen at Carlisle on trains from Newcastle.

Right: A rather grimy 'D34' 4-4-0, No 62488 *Glen Aladale*, leaves Carlisle with the 6.13pm train to Hawick in September 1959. The train has just left the LMS line at Port Carlisle Junction and is on the loop which will then cross the West Coast Main Line at Kingmoor. The diminutive Carlisle No.1 signalbox is on the left, accompanied by a vintage Caledonian signal bracket. *Glen Aladale* is probably the smallest Scottish glen to be honoured with a place among the 'D34s.' It is in fact on the western side of Loch Shiel, but the name would be found only on a large scale map. Perhaps the attractive sound of the name was a factor; in general the glens selected were those closest to NBR lines.

Below: Class J39 0-6-0 No. 64877, near Broomholm with the 10.42am train from Langholm to Riddings Junction, in May 1959. This train ran through to Carlisle. At this time most of the Langholm trains were worked by J39s. The Langholm branch closed on June 15 1964.

Above: After the withdrawal of the 'J39s' the Langholm trains were usually worked by LMS 2-6-4Ts or Ivatt 4MT 2-6-0s. In this April 1963 picture, Fowler 2-6-4T No. 42301 is in charge of the 10.42am from Langholm. The driver is trying to start the injector as he approaches Riddings Junction, with the main Waverley route metals in the foreground.

Left: Leaving Carlisle in August 1959 is 'A3' class 'Pacific' No. 60101 *Cicero* with the down 'Waverley.' The train is approaching Canal goods yard, on the Waverley route loop. The siding on the left ran to Willowholme power station, now also closed. When 'A3s' worked the 'Thames Clyde Express,' the headboard was normally mounted at the top of the smokebox, thereby hiding most of the unphotogenic double chimney when viewed from the front. It is a pity that the crews on this route did not follow the same practice! At least No. 60101 was later one of the few 'A3s' to escape the German-type smoke deflectors.

CARLISLE

Top: A busy scene at Carlisle Canal shed in June 1963, just a few days before it closed. The shed's demise followed an administrative change brought about by the opening of the new Kingmoor marshalling yard. It did not affect the motive power on the Waverley route, as the same engines, usually rostered from Edinburgh, were simply accommodated at Kingmoor. The building shown here was a combined long shed and roundhouse, although the latter was for small engines only; the main long shed was behind the 'A2,' but barely visible here because much of the roof had been removed. From the left the engines on view are: a 'WD' 2-8-0, an 'A3', two 'V2s', 'A2/3' No. 60522 *Straight Deal* and 'A3' 60041 *Salmon Trout*. For the stranger, this was a difficult shed to find - it was located just past the point at which the Silloth branch diverged from the Waverley route loop. For several years after closure the coaling tower survived as a monument to the steam era amongst the encroaching birches and willowherb; it was demolished about ten years ago.

Above: The last 'D31' 4-4-0, No. 62281 languishes at Carlisle Canal shed in April 1952. Unfortunately this very elegant locomotive was not to work again, and was officially withdrawn in December that year. It was behind this engine that I had experienced the excitement some years earlier, on the Silloth branch, of my first ever train ride. No. 62281 had the dubious distinction of being renumbered three times within five years, the first BR number of 62059 being handed over to one of the new 'K1s.' She also had the more worthy distinction of outliving at least one other member of the class by more than 20 years. No. 9736 was withdrawn in 1931.

Top: 'Princess Royal' 4-6-2 No. 46203 *Princess Margaret Rose* passes Floriston Woods with the 10am Euston-Perth service in August 1962. These woods were near Rockcliffe and about five miles north of Carlisle, by which point a fair measure of speed had been attained. The 11 coaches comprise a rather varied selection, the third vehicle being of LNER origin. Of the three 'Princess Royals' allocated to Kingmoor at the time, No. 46203 seemed to be the most likely candidate for this train.

Above: At Kingmoor shed in 1951, just a few months before withdrawal, is 4-6-0 No. 54649. Strictly an LMS engine, she was built in 1926 three years after the Grouping; the 4-6-0 was very similar to the earlier Pickersgill '60' class of the Caledonian Railway. Although classified as '4P' these engines in their final years were used exclusively on freight workings. By the end of 1953, they had gone. Although latterly hardly favourites with their crews, they were certainly among the handsomest engines to survive after Nationalisation.

Above: The changing face of Kingmoor: after the closure of Carlisle Canal shed and before the end of steam on the Waverley route, scenes such as this were not uncommon. In January 1966, 'A3' No. 60106 *Flying Fox* and 'A4' No. 60007 *Sir Nigel Gresley* stand on the north side of the shed. Edinburgh 'A3s' were common enough at Carlisle, but the appearance of 60106, a Peterborough (New England) engine, was most unusual.

Above: Despite having to contend for pride of place with a recent oil delivery, 'Princess Coronation' 4-6-2 No. 46254 *City of Stoke-on-Trent* looked so good in blue livery at Upperby in 1952 that I made what was for me a rare exposure at that time on a modern steam engine. For a brief period in the early 1950s, the 'Pacifics' on all regions and the Western Region 'Kings' were painted blue. Lack of enthusiasm from the Swindon lobby, together with the fact that blue was probably harder to keep clean, ensured a return to Brunswick green.

STEPHEN CROOK'S CLASSIC STEAM COLLECTION

Left: Upperby also hosted some rather ancient motive power, alongside its 'Duchesses', 'A4s' and 'Princess Royals.' LNWR 'Cauliflower' 0-6-0 No. 58409 comes off shed in 1953 to work an evening stopping train to Penrith. The 'Cauliflowers' in Cumberland were primarily associated with the Workington-Penrith line, but by 1951 these had been replaced by more modern engines. This locomotive is fitted with an extended cab roof and a wooden shelter over the tender, welcome refinements when working over the northern fells. The nickname of 'Cauliflower' originated from the appearance of the LNWR arms (carried on the centre wheel splasher) when seen from a distance.

Below: 'Ghost trains' that did not appear in the public timetable always had an extra fascination. The 5pm Carlisle-Dumfries workmen's train came into this category, seen here passing Port Carlisle Junction on a September day in 1959, in the charge of '2P' 4-4-0 No. 40576. Like several of the Scottish '2Ps', this engine retained its original chimney. There is no doubt that it is a Dumfries engine - to accompany the 68B shedplate on the smokebox door, the name of the depot is also painted on the bufferbeam, a practice latterly adopted by St. Rollox works in emulation of the LNER style.

Above: On Whit Monday 1964, Fowler '4F' 0-6-0 No. 44448 sweeps round the curve at Port Carlisle Junction with the 3pm to Silloth. Although it is a Bank Holiday, it is worthy of note that the train should be given eight coaches only three months before the line was closed at the end of the summer service. For several years the 'J39' 0-6-0s had worked this branch, to be followed in the early 1960s by LMS 2-6-4Ts. The use of a '4F' was rather unusual.

Below: The 10am Euston-Perth (which in 1962 had been a regular turn for a Kingmoor Class 8 'Pacific' north of Carlisle) was normally allocated to a 4-6-0 in 1963. This was frequently a Class 7P 'Royal Scot' 4-6-0, of which several examples had been transferred to Kingmoor. In this picture, No. 46157 *The Royal Artilleryman* gathers speed at Etterby Bridge, with the Down 'Perth', in August 1963.

Above: It had always been quite usual for engines to run from Kingmoor MPD to Citadel Station in pairs, or groups of three, for operating convenience. However, by 1959 – even when there was still plenty of steam – the sight had become less common. In September 1959 these three were caught at Port Carlisle Junction on their way to the station. The heterogeneous trio comprises, from the left: BR 'Standard' 4-6-0 No. 73009, Stanier 'Pacific' No. 46222 *Queen Mary*, and Gresley 'V2' class 2-6-2 No. 60834.

Left: Hellifield '2P' 4-4-0 No 40685 peeps into the sunshine at the south end of Carlisle Station in 1956, waiting to pilot the up 'Thames Clyde Express.' This picture was taken before the removal of much of the station roof, in 1958. In steam days, it was impossible to keep it even remotely clean.

Top: A very pleasant sight: Class 3F 'Jinty' 0-6-0T No 47326 engages in some vigorous shunting at the west side of Carlisle station in April 1963. By this time these engines had become the normal pilots at both ends of the station. A few years earlier, the overall roof had covered these lines too. The end of the cut-back roof can be seen at the left.

Above: Southbound departures from Carlisle were always impressive. In this view, Stanier 'Jubilee' 4-6-0 No. 45588 *Kashmir* is leaving Carlisle's No. 5 bay platform with the 4.37pm stopping train to Bradford, during

August 1964. '3F' 0-6-0T No. 47345 is rostered for south end station pilot duties. The former retaining wall at the east side of the overall roof rears up awkwardly behind the train like part of a ruined abbey. Around this time, some engines had the position of the smokebox door lamp bracket moved from the top to half-way down on the left-hand side, presumably to minimize any danger from live overhead wires. No. 45588 was one of the engines thus altered, and the effect of the new position of the single lamp denoting a stopping train is rather odd and somewhat unbalanced.

STEPHEN CROOK'S CLASSIC STEAM COLLECTION

Below: Approaching Cummersdale (the first station from Carlisle on the Cumbrian coast line) is Class 5MT 4-6-0 No. 45451, with the 2.25pm to Whitehaven, in June 1962. By this time, this was probably the last Maryport & Carlisle Railway signal still standing. In appearance it was something of a hybrid - with North British spectacle plates, but with Caledonian-type arm and finial.

Left: Thompson 'B1' 4-6-0 No. 61222 hurries along near Scotby with the 2.20pm Newcastle-Carlisle in August 1959. This was one of the faster trains on the line, taking 1hr 37min for the 60 miles trip, with seven intermediate stops. For several years the 'B1s' had been the mainstay of passenger motive power on this line. As early as 1947, I recall *Waterbuck*, *Puku*, and *Topi*, all brand-new and looking very smart in postwar-LNER green livery, gradually replacing the 'D49s.'

Below: It was always a source of frustration for 'spotters' standing on the platforms at Carlisle station that it was not possible to identify the numbers of the engines on these goods avoiding lines. It had just been possible, before Nationalisation, to read the much larger LMS and LNER numbers from the north end of the station, where the goods lines are rather nearer. Here, 'Jubilee' 4-6-0 No. 45705 *Seahorse* is seen in 1965 near Bog Junction with an up freight, passing under the West Coast Main Line, which it will shortly join. The two tracks just to the right are the goods lines for the Midland and Newcastle sections. The Midland passenger lines can be seen curving round in the distance at the right. No. 45705, a much-travelled engine, is sporting a 10B shedplate, a code taken over by Blackpool when Preston shed closed in 1961.

Right: Even when the Gresley 'A3s' took over the 'Thames Clyde Express' workings, pilots were still used occasionally. On the summer Saturday of July 16 1960, Class 5MT No. 44886 leads 'A3' No. 60038 *Firdaussi* and 11 coaches, heading out of Carlisle, past Durran Hill with the Up train. The signal on the right was the last MR lower quadrant to survive at Carlisle.

STEPHEN CROOK'S CLASSIC STEAM COLLECTION

Above: A stirring spectacle indeed: unrebuilt 'Patriot' 4-6-0 No. 45551 and a rebuilt 'Scot' 4-6-0 rattle over the points at Petteril Bridge Junction, Carlisle with the Up 'Thames Clyde Express', in December 1959. This was the point at which the Newcastle line diverged from the Midland route. The motive power was a pleasant surprise, as 'Patriots' were not regularly seen on the 'S&C.'

Below: The last days of the last 'Patriot.' No. 45530 *Sir Frank Ree* pulls out of London Road yard, Carlisle with a train for Millom in late December 1965, after a night of severe frost. This may even have been her last journey; unfortunately, I was too busy at the time to try and find out. Anyway, by December 31 1965 the class was extinct.

Right: Carlisle's diversity of motive power stemmed from the varied pre-Grouping scene. Here, Reid NBR 'N15' 0-6-2T No. 69155 shunts in London Road yard, in December 1959. A total of 99 of these engines were built from 1910 as a development of the earlier 'N14s.' London Road yard was adjacent to the Carlisle-Newcastle line, being originally the NER goods yard. Until the early 1960s, it was usually shunted by NBR engines from Canal shed. After the opening of the new Kingmoor marshalling yard in 1963, all Carlisle's separate yards, a legacy from the days when the city was served by seven different companies, became redundant.

STEPHEN CROOK'S CLASSIC STEAM COLLECTION

Top: Probably the most attractive remaining main line steam working on summer Saturdays in 1967 was the relief to the northbound 'Thames Clyde Express', which was regularly worked between Leeds and Carlisle by a Holbeck 'Jubilee.' A public-spirited group of amateur cleaners ensured that the engines were usually in sparkling condition! In this picture 'Jubilee' 4-6-0 No. 45562 *Alberta* is passing the site of Carlisle London Road yard with the 9.45am goods to Stourton on Saturday September 2 1967. This engine had worked north the previous Saturday on the relief 'Thames Clyde,' but had spent most of the week in Kingmoor repair shop. The position of the Cathedral and the Castle on the skyline is a reminder that the 'S&C' runs east-west at this point.

Above: NBR 'J35' 0-6-0 No. 64499 stands at the south end of London Road yard, Carlisle, in April 1959. These engines were an earlier and rather more elegant version of the 'J37' class. By this time, No. 64499 was the only one of the class still working from Canal shed.

Right: 'Standard' Class 9F 2-10-0 No. 92017 runs light past Durran Hill Junction Box in December 1967. This was one of the original '9Fs', with a single chimney, built in 1954. It was withdrawn in December 1967 and scrapped after a working life of just 13 years. What a waste!

Above: Nominal pioneer 'Jubilee' 4-6-0 No. 45552 *Silver Jubilee* leaves Carlisle with the Edinburgh-Birmingham train (1M23) during January 1960. This engine was named in honour of the Silver Jubilee of King George V in 1935, and in addition received a special black livery embellished with many chromium-plated parts. The cabside numerals and tender lettering were in relief characters. The one aspect of this splendid livery that survived into BR days was the raised cabside numbers which were recast in normal BR style. In this photograph they survive, but even these were removed shortly afterwards. In the summer and at holiday times, as here, the Edinburgh-Birmingham and Glasgow-Birmingham trains ran as separate trains instead of being combined at Carstairs. The reporting number for the former was 1M23, and for the latter 1M25. These were usually displayed on the engine, particularly as the trains ran only ten minutes apart: the Edinburgh-Birmingham was due out of Carlisle at 12.20pm, and the Glasgow-Birmingham at 12.30pm. The engine was withdrawn in September 1964.

STEPHEN CROOK'S CLASSIC STEAM COLLECTION

Above: This stretch of line, south of Wreay station, was a favourite photographic spot for midday trains, as the line curved, allowing the sun to strike the train at a more favourable angle. The unrelieved ascent from Carlisle also meant that trains were still moving fairly slowly. On Easter Monday 1961, rebuilt 'Patriot' 4-6-0 No. 45526 *Morecambe and Heysham*, recently ex-works, is going well with the Glasgow-Birmingham (1M25). The two through coaches to the Western Region are still in chocolate and cream livery.

Above: An up freight at Brisco bridge, two miles south of Carlisle in August 1964, hauled by Edge Hill 'Crab' 2-6-0 No. 42886. George Hughes and Henry Fowler collaborated to produce this class, ultimately of 245 engines, in 1926.

Above: Stanier 'Pacific' No. 46245 *City of London* approaches Wreay with the up 'Birmingham' in December 1959. At this time there was an ER 'B17' with the same name, though it was withdrawn a few months later. Until this time I had tended to press the shutter with the train at some distance. This made it easier to have most of the train in focus and avoided motion blur; it also gave a slightly telephoto effect. This time I let the train come nearer, and this picture represents the whole negative. The engine is sharp, but the perspective is steeper than usual - rather too steep for my taste, but a pleasant picture for all that!

Left: Climbing to Wreay with the up 'Perth' on a hot, hazy day in May 1959 is No. 46238 *City of Carlisle*. This is the only picture I have of this engine, despite it being based at Upperby most of its life! Upperby seemed to work diagrams all over the LMR, and engines could be away for several days. A visit to Upperby shed might reveal only a small part of the allocation.

Above: The combined Edinburgh and Glasgow-Birmingham train, seen about a mile south of the Carlisle city boundary in January 1961, with Stanier 'Pacific' No. 46248 *City of Leeds* in charge. A good deal of steam from the carriage heating system seems to be going to waste from under the first coach. In the winter months, with GMT representing the actual time, the sun was an hour 'further round.' This was to the photographer's advantage with these mid-day trains. A splendid sight!

Right: The 'Duchess' in decline: LMS 'Pacific' No. 46230 *Duchess of Buccleuch* approaches the long-closed station at Brisco, on the climb out of Carlisle with the 4pm (SuO) milk train to London (Wood Lane) in September 1963. On weekdays, the milk wagons were attached to the rear of one of the expresses, usually the 'Midday Scot.'

STEPHEN CROOK'S CLASSIC STEAM COLLECTION

Top: Double-chimneyed Riddles '9F' 2-10-0 No 92212 trundles under the bridge just north of Wreay station with an up soda ash train comprising 11 vehicles.

Above: A very long freight struggles out of Carlisle behind Class 8P No. 46233 *Duchess of Sutherland*, in August 1963. The first six vehicles are loaded cattle wagons. Even in their last sad days, it was not very usual to see 'Duchesses' on this sort of working.

Below: The up 'Thames Clyde Express', unfortunately not carrying a headboard, is seen near Cotehill, six miles south of Carlisle, on Easter Monday 1961. The station here had been closed on April 7 1952. The 'A3' in charge, No. 60036 *Colombo*, was not one of the more common members of the class to appear on this train - it is carrying a 55H (Neville Hill) shedplate. The usual motive power was a Holbeck (55A) 'A3.'

STEPHEN CROOK'S CLASSIC STEAM COLLECTION

NORTH EAST ENGLAND

Above: 'K1' 2-6-0 No. 62021 has a mid-day break at Alnwick in May 1966, just a few weeks before steam operation ceased on the branch to Alnmouth. The large and impressive NER station, built in 1887, was probably for the benefit of important people who had come to visit the Duke of Northumberland at Alnwick Castle. Although there were only two platforms, the station was equipped with many extra refinements. Note the glass platform screens just in front of the engine - an attempt to make the station a little less draughty. On the right can be seen the top of the monument erected in 1816 to the Second Duke of Northumberland and which supports the Percy lion. The branch closed to passenger traffic in January 1968, and to freight in October 1968.

Left: Class J21 0-6-0 No. 65033 approaches Knowesgate with a westbound ballast train in August 1959. This was the first station on the Bellingham line after Scotsgap Junction (written as Scotsgap on the station signs, but as Scots Gap nearly everywhere else!) There were several other small bridges on the line that looked almost identical to this one. The 'J21s' looked similar to the 'J25s', but with their larger driving wheels (5ft 1.25in as opposed to 4ft 7.25in) they were basically passenger engines. No. 65033 is the 'J21' now preserved at the North of England Open Air Museum, at Beamish.

Right: Goods engines cluster round one of the turntables, at Borough Gardens shed, Gateshead; note the the smoke vents, slender columns and vaulting girders in the roof. The engines are, left to right: 'J27' 0-6-0 No. 65823, 'Q6' 0-8-0 No. 63408, and 'J25 0-6-0 No. 65728. All the engines are at home, as indicated by their 52J shedplates. The main shed at Gateshead (52A) was not more than a half-mile away, but it dealt mainly with passenger engines, while Borough Gardens housed the freight locomotives. There was a further point of difference for unauthorised visitors (with whom of course I would hasten to disassociate myself!) - Gateshead was not easy of access, being surrounded on three sides by busy tracks, and on the other by a steep bank down to the Tyne; Borough Gardens, on the other hand, presented no problems at all.......

Above: When I returned to England in the Autumn of 1958, after three months abroad, I found that even in that short time things had changed for the worse. I realised that if, for example, I wanted an action shot of a 'G5' 0-4-4T there was no time to lose. The Sunderland-South Shields push-pull was the only working I could discover where one was still active. So, after listening to the weather forecast for the next day, I arrived at Sunderland late one afternoon in early November. To my dismay, I saw that the train from South Shields was running bunker first. There are few more unpromising situations than a push-pull working where the front of the engine is coupled to the coaches! However, the

shedmaster at Sunderland generously offered to have the engine turned - as indeed I had hoped he might! I was rather short of money, so I spent the night at a Salvation Army dormitory in Sunderland for about 1/6. At least there was no temptation to lie-in! Fortunately, the next morning was sunny, if a little hazy. I took a train out to East Boldon, north of which the line curvature seemed from the map to be at a more favourable angle. I walked about a mile up the line and photographed the next northbound train. This is the result of my efforts. The engine is 'G5' 0-4-4T No. 67253, for many years a regular engine on the Harrogate-Boroughbridge push-pull service.

Left: Typical Tyneside terraces look down on South Shields station, where Sunderland 'N10' 0-6-2T No. 69101 has just arrived with a parcels train in November 1958. A total of 20 of these engines were built by Worsdell in 1902, for the NER.

Above: One of the most attractive steam workings in the north east to survive in 1967 was the service to Silksworth colliery, which joined the Sunderland-Seaham line at Ryhope. These trains were worked by Sunderland 'J27' 0-6-0s, which were usually in good external condition. No. 65879 climbs towards Silksworth with a train of empty wagons on August 31 1967.

Above: By the summer of 1959, it was very difficult to find any 'A8' class 4-6-2Ts still at work, but on Durham miners' gala day on Saturday July 18 it was a different story, and as usual, 'everything with wheels' was pressed into service. Many extra local trains were worked, and passenger trains even ran to Waterhouses, a village six miles west of Durham – the only day in the year that this occurred. In this picture, an evening empty stock train from Sunderland, hauled by 'A8' 4-6-2T No. 69850, is about to join the main line two miles north of Durham, whence it will transport late revellers back to Wearside. From the photographer's point of view, the train has arrived in the 'nick of time', for the creeping shadow from the embankment on which I am standing is just about to engulf the far track.

Right, upper: Condemned at Darlington! 'J77' 0-6-0T No. 8417 in the works scrapyard in 1950. With outside springs over the front wheels, these engines had a delightfully antiquated appearance. They were Worsdell rebuilds of Fletcher 0-4-4Ts built circa 1880.

Right, lower: One of the last 'J24' 0-6-0s, No. 65617, stands in the rain at Darlington scrapyard in 1951. This was one of the NER engines that worked in Scotland, being allocated to St. Margarets. The 'J24s' looked similar to the 'J25s', but with a shorter wheelbase.

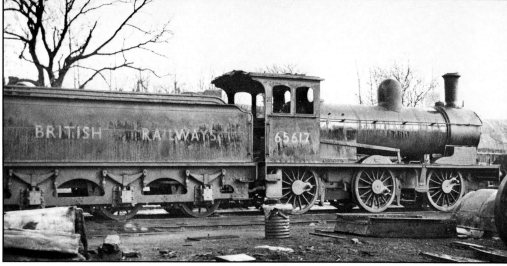

STEPHEN CROOK'S CLASSIC STEAM COLLECTION

PENRITH, SHAP & ROUTES SOUTH

Left: Unrebuilt 'Patriot' 4-6-0 No. 45513 passes Calthwaite signalbox with the 4.13pm from Carlisle to Preston and Manchester on August 2 1961. This was a slow train, and with an official stopping time of either 3 or 4 minutes at every station which it served, it was not booked to reach Preston until 6.32pm. The engine is carrying a Carnforth shedplate, but before it was withdrawn in September 1962 it had been transferred to Edge Hill. Calthwaite box also disappeared shortly afterwards.

Below: The fireman has clearly been building up his fire for the climb to Blencow, as Ivatt '2MT' 2-6-0 No 46432 leaves Penrith in August 1964 with the down Workington portion of the 'Lakes Express.' The train, which left Euston at 11.20am, contains a through coach due to arrive at Workington at 7.53pm. The train ran for a short summer season only - from the end of June until the end of August.

Above: Unrebuilt 'Patriot' 4-6-0 No. 45505 *Royal Army Ordnance Corps* recovers from a signal check near Calthwaite with a down freight on August 2 1961. This engine is coupled to a high-sided tender, which had previously been paired with 'Patriot' No. 45551. No. 45505 was one of the 'Patriots' which received a military name after the last war, having previously been un-named. The engine ended its days with a brief spell at Lancaster Green Ayre, from where it would have worked trains mainly on the line to Leeds. It was withdrawn in June 1962.

Above: The first LMS 'Pacific,' No. 46200 *The Princess Royal,* hurries past between Penrith and Clifton with the up 'Birmingham' in August 1961. At the time this was the up train most likely to have a 'Lizzie' on the front. This fine locomotive was withdrawn in November 1962 and reduced to scrap by Connell's of Coatbridge.

Left: A rather run-down Class 5MT 4-6-0, No 45072, emerges from the bridges at Clifton at the start of the northern climb to Shap summit on July 25 1967. The train is the summer Saturdays 1.26pm Glasgow-Morecambe. In monochrome, the new-liveried blue and grey coach seemingly indicates a return to the old red and cream colours!

Right: Climbing through the picturesque woods north of Thrimby Grange on the northern side of Shap is Hughes/Fowler 'Crab' 2-6-0 No. 42846, at the head of an up freight in September 1964. As a Gorton (9G) engine, it would be a rather unusual visitor to the area, and by this time the class was quickly disappearing. There is considerable super-elevation on the track along this tortuous section, to facilitate fast downhill running. The trees along this stretch have since been felled, giving a very different appearance to the area.

Above: A stirring sight for lovers of LMS locomotives: Fowler unrebuilt 'Patriot' 4-6-0 No 45550 of Carnforth shed forges towards Shap summit on August 6 1962, with an up empty stock train. I was out of bed early that morning to give me as much time as possible to clean the engine. It should have been half-an-hour earlier, as unfortunately there was no help available on this occasion! Even my 6ft 3in stature did not enable me to reach the whole dome! I also never managed to start the tender. No. 45550 was the last of the unrebuilt 'Patriots' to be withdrawn, by December 1962, just four months after this picture was taken. It doesn't look ready for the scrapheap, does it?

Above: Shap Summit. 'Britannia' class 'Pacific' No. 70042 *Lord Roberts* passes in August 1963 with the 1.10pm Euston-Glasgow. The maroon-liveried train features both LMS and BR Mk. 1 vehicles. The other steam engine in the picture, at Shap Granite works, was rather less impressive – a small industrial saddle tank.

Left: Rebuilt 'Royal Scot' 4-6-0 No. 46118 *Royal Welch Fusilier* approaches Shap summit with the 1.10pm Euston-Glasgow, during August 1963.

Top: In December 1967, '9F' 2-10-0 No. 92017 hurries north light engine at Shap Wells, while a diesel-hauled express, led by a Class 47 diesel electric, heads south down the bank. This picture was taken about one mile from the summit. Tebay is around three miles down the hill.

Above: The last days of steam on Shap Fell: in late December 1967, an unidentified Stanier Class 5MT 4-6-0 heads north near Shap Wells with a very mixed freight, which includes a 'dead' LMS Ivatt 4MT 'Mogul.' 'Standard' 4-6-0 No 75026 is assisting at the rear.

STEPHEN CROOK'S CLASSIC STEAM COLLECTION

Above: 'Standard' Class 4MT 4-6-0 No. 75026 assists a freight on Shap Fell in December 1967, just a few days before the end of steam in the area. The double chimney indicates that this engine was one of the later batch, introduced in 1957. It is carrying BR green livery, a legacy of the engine's days on the Western Region. This broadside view clearly shows a practice common on BR: leaving the tank filler lid open!

Below: The permanent way cabin at Greenholme must have been one of the most photographed structures of its kind in the country. It was situated around three-quarters of a mile north of Tebay, on the four-miles haul to the summit of the 1 in 75 climb, and thus an ideal location at which to photograph trains working hard. Britannia 'Pacific' No 70039 *Sir Christopher Wren* climbs past with a down Manchester express on a warm, hazy day in August 1963.

Above: The Lune Gorge, south of Tebay, was a majestic photographic location before the intrusive and noisy M6 shouldered through, alongside the railway. Britannia Pacific No 70016, formerly named *Ariel*, but now running without nameplates, leads a modest northbound freight towards the troughs at Dillicar in August 1967.

STEPHEN CROOK'S CLASSIC STEAM COLLECTION

Left: In August 1950, the roofless shed at Workington is host to an LNWR Webb 'Cauliflower' 0-6-0 of 1887. This was the last year these engines worked over the 'CKP' line through the heart of the Lake District, via Keswick, as the LMS Ivatt 2-6-0s were by this stage taking over most of their duties.

Above: Another pre-Grouping survivor: Furness Railway Pettigrew '3F' 0-6-0 No. 12494, at Moor Row shed in 1949. This engine retains its original FR boiler; of the few engines that survived the war only one carried an original boiler – but it was not always the same engine. At one stage, No. 12494 certainly had an LYR boiler. Moor Row was three miles south-east of Whitehaven.

Right: FR 0-6-0 No. 12499 stands at the coaling plant at its home shed, Workington, in 1949. The LYR boiler with which she has been fitted looks much less distinguished than the original Furness type.

Above: Unrebuilt 'Patriot' 4-6-0 No 45543 *Home Guard* approaches Cark and Cartmel with the 12.20pm Barrow-Carnforth in August 1962. It is interesting to note that this engine was officially named in July 1940, in the early months of the war; it was withdrawn in November 1962 and scrapped at Crewe Works in September 1963.

STEPHEN CROOK'S CLASSIC STEAM COLLECTION

Top: Class 5MT 4-6-0 No. 45072 and '9F' Crosti-boilered 2-10-0 No. 92024 pass Clapham, Yorkshire, with the tanks from Heysham to the north east in May 1967. In 1955, ten BR '9F' 2-10-0s were fitted with Franco-Crosti boilers as an experimental coal-saving measure. It was not a success.

Above: Period of transition: Type 2 diesel No. D5170 and '9F' 2-10-0 No. 92167 climb from Bentham with the Heysham tanks train in April 1968. No. 92167 was one of three examples in the class fitted with a mechanical stoker.

THE SETTLE-CARLISLE LINE

Above: The driver (and doubtless the fireman) has Ais Gill summit gratefully in sight after 45 miles of almost continuous climbing from Carlisle. Stanier '8F' 2-8-0 No 48090 is passing Mallerstang with an up freight on November 4 1967. As a Newton Heath (9D) engine, it was a rather unusual visitor to 'the Long Drag.'

Right: An easy climb: '5MT' 4-6-0 No. 44886 not surprisingly makes light work of the load which on this occasion in August 1967 was the 1.4pm goods from Carlisle to Skipton. The impressive background of Wild Boar Fell makes this one of the best known views on the 'S&C.' It is about half-a-mile north of Ais Gill summit, which reaches a height of 1,169ft above sea level, making it the highest main line summit in England. Unfortunately, from the photographer's point of view it also makes it one of the cloudiest! This can be seen here, as even on a predominantly sunny day, threatening cloud shadows dapple the hill behind.

Top: A view which, for me, says a great deal about the Midland line through the Fells. A class 5MT 4-6-0 draws into the loop at Blea Moor with a northbound freight on October 4 1967. This three-mile stretch embraces the two most striking railway landmarks on the line, with Ribblehead Viaduct to the south and Blea Moor tunnel to the north. In this picture, the tunnel entrance is out of sight round the curve in the distance.

Above: Between Ribblehead and Blea Moor, an unidentified '8F' 2-8-0 heads north on October 4 1967, with empty anhydrite wagons from Widnes to the Long Meg gypsum mine, near Little Salkeld. The parapet of the famous Batty Moss Viaduct can just be seen above the middle of the train. In the background at the right is Park Fell, one of the foothills of Ingleborough.

Below: LMS Class 4P 'Compound' 4-4-0 No. 41113 leaves Hellifield on a November afternoon in 1958 with the 12.30pm departure from Morecambe to Leeds City. The line on the left runs to Daisyfield Junction, at Blackburn. By the end of 1958, after wholesale withdrawals in previous months, active 'Compounds' suddenly became scarce. Even at Lancaster Green Ayre, only two remained, and a phone call to the shed was a prerequisite for both trips I made to the area at this time. On the first occasion, having discovered that No. 41113 was due to leave Morecambe at 12.30pm the next day, I travelled to Lancaster. However despite a good forecast, the weather was cloudy just before the train was due to leave. As I did not have my own transport at this time, I was forced to fall back on my policy of 'If you cannot photograph it, join it'. I therefore boarded the train, with the intention of alighting and taking a departure shot at the first station where the sun was shining, assuming there were no other snags. However as station after station went by with still no sign of the sun, my hopes of any success that day were quickly disappearing. I reckoned that Hellifield would be my last chance, for after that the sun would be too low anyway. Finally, at the last possible moment, my perseverance paid off. The sun just managed to shine until the train had left the station. Lucky for once!

Right: Stanier '5XP' 4-6-0 'Jubilee' class 4-6-0 No. 45581 *Bihar and Orissa* passes her home shed, at Farnley Junction, with a Leeds-Blackpool 'extra' on Whit Monday, 1966.

LANCASHIRE

With the lofty spire of St Walburge's Roman Catholic church standing between the Blackpool and Carlisle routes, north of Preston, Stanier '8F' 2-8-0 No. 48423 takes the up main line at Preston with an evening freight from Fleetwood, comprised largely of tank wagons from the ICI factory at Thornton, in May 1968. The foundations of Preston shed can still be seen on the left; it was destroyed by fire and closed in September 1961.

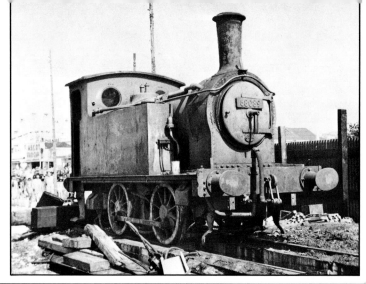

Right: Strolling down the 'prom' at Morecambe one day in August 1955, I was very surprised to come across this LNER 'Y7' being used during alterations to the seafront. Fortunately, I happened to have my camera with me. The smokebox door still carries the number 68089 and a Tweedmouth shedplate (52D). The dome has not been removed - this engine never had one! Its previous job for BR was to work the three-miles branch from Chathill to Seahouses on the Northumberland coast, closed in October 1951.

Below: The finest signal gantry in the country still standing at the end of the BR steam era must have been this one, just north of the Preston station. In May 1968, '8F' 2-8-0 No. 48765 trundles beneath the serried semaphores with a train of BR standard 16-ton capacity mineral wagons.

Right: On 28 March 1968, Stanier '8F' 2-8-0 No. 48384 passes Kirkham with a coal train for Burn Naze. This is a reminder that Kirkham was, until the mid-1960s, a three-way junction for the three routes to Blackpool. By 1968, the lines in the foreground (formerly to Blackpool Central) were merely sidings. The two lines furthest from the camera run to Blackpool North (via Poulton) and Fleetwood, while the tracks curving off on the right (behind the signals) go to Blackpool South (via St Annes) Ironically, the closed line to Blackpool Central was far more direct and twice as fast as either of the other two routes, but as it served no intermediate stations, it was the one that had to go. It closed in November 1964.

Below: The crews of two '8Fs' shunting at Kirkham enjoy a mid-day chat by the lineside as a sister '8F' 2-8-0 steams past with a coal train for Burn Naze power station, at Fleetwood. It is May 1968 and steam's day is almost done; by August, it was all over. All the engines are very dirty and the piles of track show that several of the sidings are being lifted. Chalked on the tenderside of the '8F' on the left (No.48282) is the football result 'Man Utd 1 Man City 3.'

Left: LYR Barton Wright 0-6-0ST No. 11394, seen at Horwich Works in 1952. Five of these engines were allocated to the Service Department at Horwich, and all retained their LMS numbers until withdrawal. They acquired a BR crest on the tanksides and BR type numerals on the cab, but their distinctive LMS-style numberplates survived until they went for scrap.

Above: A delightful scene at Horwich station. Aspinall LYR 2-4-2T (of 1889) No. 50647 awaits the rightaway in June 1958 with the 8.30am push-pull train to Blackrod. The engine was replaced by more modern steam power shortly afterwards. This branch was just over one mile in length, making it one of the shortest in the country. It closed on September 27 1965.

Right: Visits to Works often produced remarkable sightings. Here, Webb LNWR 0-4-2 box tank No. 7865 is pictured in the yard at Crewe on a murky day in 1949. The locomotive was built in 1901, and still carries its LMS number. The shunting capstans, then still a relatively common sight in goods yards and depots, are certainly in keeping with the vintage of the locomotive.

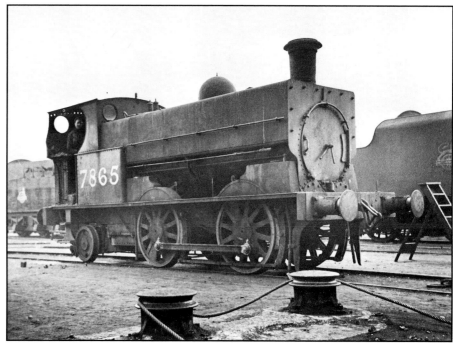

STEPHEN CROOK'S CLASSIC STEAM COLLECTION

NORTH YORKSHIRE

Above: 'Q1' class 0-8-0T No 69928 at Northallerton in August 1959. These engines were a Thompson 1942 rebuild of Robinson's 'Q4' 0-8-0 tender engine. In 1947, they were designated by the LNER as a standard class, but in the event no further engines were produced, the number in the class therefore remaining at 13. Before Nationalisation, they had the unique distinction of carrying a brass plate on the side of the bunker featuring the letters LNER, instead of having them painted or transferred onto the tank side in the normal way.

Left: The last 'A2' class 'Pacific', No. 60539 *Bronzino,* at Ripon in August 1959 with the 8.55am Newcastle-Liverpool train. This engine represents the double-chimney variety of the Peppercorn 'A2.' The platforms at Ripon were not long enough to accommodate express trains, with the result that the engine is standing on the viaduct.

Right: The stiff climb to Monkton Moor lies ahead of this ageing 'J39' 0-6-0 as it leaves Ripon viaduct with a heavy southbound freight in August 1959. The engine is No. 64845, of Starbeck shed. The lower quadrant signal is a fine example of the NER slotted post variety.

Above: The hills of North Yorkshire meant that double-heading was fairly common around Harrogate, but the combination of a 'D49' 4-4-0 and a 'WD' 2-8-0 was nevertheless rather a striking spectacle. No. 62759 *The Craven* and No. 90426 are ascending the 1 in 66 climb from Dragon Junction to Harrogate station, with a permanent way materials train in August 1959.

Below: The engine shed serving Harrogate was at Starbeck, 1.5 miles east of the town; this is the west end of the shed in August 1959. It was situated in the fork between the line to York curving away to the left, and the old connecting line to Pannal Junction at the right, which had been closed by this time. The shed itself was closed by the end of 1959. On display here are 'D49' No 62738 *The Zetland,* accompanied by 'J39' and 'J25' 0-6-0s.

Left: The first 'D49/2' 'Hunt' class 4-4-0 No. 62736 *The Bramham Moor,* leaving York in 1952 with a Harrogate train. The first coach looks delightfully antiquated, but I do not think many of us really appreciated the rolling stock in those days!

THE MIDLANDS

Above: The 6.7am Sheffield (Victoria)-Nottingham (Victoria) train leaves Tibshelf Town in July 1959 in spirited style in the charge of 'D11' Director 4-4-0 No. 62660 *Butler Henderson.* The engine was withdrawn a few months later. In this picture, the coupling rod is almost hidden beneath the splasher, so that from that point of view I should have released the shutter a second earlier or a second later. Most people agree, particularly with this sort of engine, that the rods look best in the downward position – official photographs are usually thus posed. However, I do not believe anyone who says they can consciously guarantee to photograph a moving train with the rods down! The figure on the platform to the left of the lamp post is the station mistress. When I returned to the platform, instead of delivering the expected reproach, she insisted I stayed for a very welcome cup of tea! *Butler Henderson* survives today as part of the National Collection, at Loughborough, on the Great Central Railway.

Right: At a time when most of the 'Jinty' 0-6-0Ts had been withdrawn from normal service, Williamthorpe Colliery near Chesterfield was still making use of some of these engines. All retained their BR numbers. Here, the traffic lights give a clear road to No. 47629 whilst shunting in September 1967.

Above: One of the last active 'Compounds', No. 41157, accompanies a rebuilt 'Patriot' 4-6-0, passing High Peak Junction at speed with a down Manchester express in May 1959. The Cromford & High Peak mineral line ran north-west from here to join the Buxton-Ashbourne line at Parsley Hay.

Left: The GCR's 4-6-2Ts were impressive engines. 'A5' No. 69808 is seen near Burton Joyce with a Lincoln-Nottingham parcels train, during May 1959. This was one of the original Robinson engines, introduced in 1911.

THE MIDLANDS

STEPHEN CROOK'S CLASSIC STEAM COLLECTION

Facing page: MR 0-4-4T No 58065 is in charge of the Southwell-Rolleston Junction push-pull train in May 1959. The engine was a Johnson design of 1881. The location is about half-way along the two-miles branch. On Saturdays there was a frequent service all day, while on other weekdays there was a three-hour gap in the middle of the day. Like many trains of this sort, it did not operate on Sundays. It did not in fact operate much longer at all, for within a few months of this picture the service was withdrawn, at the end of the 1959 summer service.

Above: It was well worth travelling long distances to photograph railways like this. No. 58148, a Johnson '2F' 0-6-0 built in 1876, pulls away from Glenfield with the mid-day freight from Leicester West Bridge station to Desford Junction in March 1963. Not many branch line delights survived as long as this, but fortunately, larger engines were not allowed through Glenfield tunnel. Once, this had been a common class, but by 1963 only three engines remained, all allocated to Coalville at Leicester. Fortunately, the train had been shunting for about 20 minutes at Glenfield, allowing me to take one picture of the train emerging from the tunnel, then to walk round and take this second shot.

Left: In the heart of rural Rutland, MR 0-6-0T No. 47250 meanders along near Bisbrooke, on the Seaton Junction-Uppingham branch, with an afternoon train on October 5 1959. Normally, the motive power for this branch was provided by Peterborough Spital Bridge shed in the form of a 4-4-2 'Tilbury Tank,' but on this occasion an engine had been borrowed from Leicester (15C). It is one of the original Johnson 0-6-0Ts, forerunners of the LMS 'Jinties'. This engine probably looks more suited to a one-coach train than the larger LTS tank. In its later days the branch was worked by a modern Ivatt 2-6-2T.

PETERBOROUGH, MARCH & KING'S LYNN

Right: Approaching Essendine with a train from Stamford in May 1958, is GNR 'C12' 4-4-2T No. 67394. To connect with the East Coast Main Line, this branch ran north-east, partly because of the curvature of the main line at this point, and partly because it would be likely to be used only by people going north. Travellers going south from Stamford would normally use the old LMS line to Peterborough.

Below: By the summer of 1960, King's Lynn was perhaps the best place to see the most interesting GER survivors working out their last days. Only one active 'B12' remained, and although it was a Norwich engine, on this occasion it had been sent to King's Lynn to stand in for a missing diesel on the Hunstanton service. The timetable had an ominous 'D' (diesel) at the head of the relevant column, but I hope the passengers felt as little disappointment as I did at the change of motive power. In this picture, No 61572 swings round through the attractive avenue of trees on the northern approach to King's Lynn with the 5.18pm from Hunstanton, in May 1960. A fine trio of LNER coaches complete the scene, the last two being articulated vehicles. This locomotive survives on the North Norfolk Railway.

STEPHEN CROOK'S CLASSIC STEAM COLLECTION

Above: Another last survivor, 'D16' 4-4-0 No. 62613, leaves Kings Lynn with the 11.43am to Wisbech and March, in May 1960. This was another train preceded by a 'D' in an over-optimistic timetable. This train would follow the main line south to Ely for six miles, then would turn off at Magdalen Road and head due west for Wisbech. In their last days, BR steam engines were either filthy or else particularly well-maintained – one extreme or the other! Fortunately, these fine GER engines fell into the latter category. No. 62613 is carrying a March (31B) shedplate, and it was from the same shed that the engine was withdrawn in October 1960.

Above: Vintage GER motive power at work. 'J17' 0-6-0 No. 65577 pilots 'J69' 0-6-0T No. 68499 leaving leafy Lynn in May 1960 with the regular mid-day sand train to Middleton Towers. This was the first station out of King's Lynn on the line to Swaffham. Both these engines were introduced by J. Holden at the turn of the century - the 'J17s' in 1900, and the 'J69s' in 1902, so they certainly gave value for money.

Right: 'K3' 2-6-0 No. 61954 takes the Peterborough line out of March with a permanent way train in December 1960. I had to include this photograph because, surprisingly, it is my only picture of a 'K3.' They were not our favourite engines at this time, because in so many cases they had replaced older and more interesting classes, and also they were so common that there seemed to be no urgency about photographing them. Even this one was only taken while I was waiting for something else. There were nearly 200 members of the class, but before the end of 1963 all the 'K3s' had gone.

Above: Electricity is the main theme in the background, but fortunately the motive power for this up express, leaving Peterborough in June 1964, is still steam. The engine is 'A1' class 'Pacific' No. 60156 *Great Central.* The five engines of this class whose names commemorated the five major pre-Grouping companies of the LNER all carried the company crest above the nameplate. No. 60156 was also one of the only four engines in the class to be fitted with roller bearings. The locomotive was withdrawn in April 1965 and stored at York until October of the same year, when it was despatched to Clayton & Davie's yard at Dunston on Tyne, and scrapped in the following month.

Above: In May 1964, Thompson 'B1' 4-6-0 No. 61205 emerges from beneath the distinctive signalbox at Peterborough East, with a Leicester train. The box would provide the best possible visibility, but one would have thought it might have been just too much of a good thing for the signalman! A green-liveried English Electric diesel stands in the platform, awaiting departure.

Left: A lightweight down express comprised of just five BR Standard Mk 1 coaches leaves St. Neots, on the slow line in May 1960, behind 'A3' class 'Pacific' No. 60047 *Donovan*. The double-chimneyed engine is also paired with a GNR-style railed tender, rather than the more modern Gresley-built variety.

CAMBRIDGE

Above: Royal engines also had to work everyday trains like any other locomotive, and 'B2' 4-6-0 No. 61671 *Royal Sovereign* regularly worked the 3.15pm Cambridge-King's Cross. It is seen here in its usual immaculate condition, leaving Cambridge with this train in March 1958. After three miles the train left the main line to Liverpool Street, and ran south west to meet the GNR main line at Hitchin. On the left are the lines to Bletchley and Oxford. No. 61671 was one of ten 'B17' class 'Sandringhams' rebuilt as 'B2s.' It was originally named *Manchester City,* but was renamed shortly after rebuilding and given a name more fitting for a royal engine. When No. 61671 was withdrawn in September 1958, the nameplate and royal engine status were transferred to another 'B2,' No. 61632. However this engine also was condemned five months later.

Right: Ex-Works B12 4-6-0 No 61577 of Ipswich shed (32B) forges away from Cambridge with an up breakdown train in 1957. As Ipswich engines did not usually appear at Cambridge, this is probably a running-in turn. The building on the left is the old LNWR engine shed, which had been closed for several years.

Left: Of the splendid selection of engines still seen at Cambridge until the late 1950s, the 'E4s' were the icing on the cake. Their delightfully antiquated appearance, and the fact that they easily outlasted all the other 2-4-0 tender engines in the country made them a real anachronism. No. 62789 is in charge of the 1.19pm to Colchester, leaving Cambridge, in 1957.

Below: Seen here in rather grubby condition is 'Sandringham' No. 61672 *West Ham United.* Although numerically adjacent to *Royal Sovereign,* any other similarities between the two engines as shown here and on the previous page are not immediately obvious. Apart from the fact that No. 61672 is an original 'B17', the difference in external condition could hardly be more pronounced. In view of the proximity of Upton Park to Stratford, the home shed of 61672, I was surprised that this engine often seemed to be the dirtiest of the 'Footballers' in the allocation. Perhaps there was some local rivalry. In this picture, 61672 pulls out under Hills Road bridge with a Sunday afternoon train to Liverpool Street, in May 1957. Most surprisingly, for this late date, the train consists entirely of GER stock. As a further point of difference compared with No. 61671, this engine is carrying express passenger discs instead of headlamps, as she is running over GER lines to Liverpool Street. This of course would not apply to the King's Cross route.

Above: The crew show off the curvaceous lines of their engine while engaged in station pilot duties at Cambridge, in 1957. The locomotive is 'D16/3' 4-4-0 No. 62592, and this picture clearly shows the attractive footplating over the wheels, which was retained by some of the class. The life story of 62592 reads: built in 1910, became 'D16/2' in 1929, converted to 'D16/3' in 1945, withdrawn April 1958.

Facing page, lower: 'D16/3' 4-4-0 No 62606, recently ex-Works, stands in one of the bay platforms at the north end of Cambridge station, leading a local train to King's Lynn, in 1956. The main line platform on the left still has the distinction of being the longest BR platform contained within a single station. The location of the shed could almost have been designed with trainspotters in mind, and the boy on the platform was in the right position to take advantage of it: the dark area at the right is actually part of the MPD!

Left: The veteran 'J15' 0-6-0s worked some of the Colchester line trains. In 1957, No. 65461 leaves Cambridge station with the 1.19 pm service. The question of whether discs or head-lamps were used appeared to be purely arbitrary, no doubt depending on availability. The old goods shed can be seen on the right.

Right: At Cambridge the goods line ran just to the east of the station, but rejoined the passenger lines shortly thereafter. Here, an Up freight is about to rejoin the main line. The engine is Class O1 2-8-0 No. 63784, from March shed. Originally a Robinson GCR design, it was rebuilt by Thompson in 1944 with a new boiler, Walschaerts valve gear and new cylinders.

Below: An interesting scene at the north end of Cambridge station in May 1960. 'Britannia' 'Pacific' No. 70011 *Hotspur* is waiting to depart with the 8.20am (SuO) Liverpool Street to Norwich. The fine GER signal bracket survived well into the 1960s. Note the other semaphore gantries at the south end of the station. On the right, two 'B1' 4-6-0s (No. 61043 leading) are standing outside the shed.

Above: A pleasing portrait of 'E4' 2-4-0 No. 62797, at Cambridge shed in 1957, shortly after the engine's transfer from Lowestoft. This picture shows the enlarged cab and tender-cab with which six engines in the class were fitted. These presumably were the 'E4s' strangely transferred to Darlington in the 1930s for working across the Pennines to Penrith.

Above: 'B17/6' 4-6-0 No. 61636 *Harlaxton Manor* under the coaling plant at Cambridge shed in 1956. In those days I was far more likely to photo-graph those 'Sandringhams' that retained their original smokebox doors (as seen here) as I thought they looked much better than the later bevelled variety, without the flange round the edge. I always regarded the smokebox door as the 'face' of the locomotive, and any changes to this immediately altered its overall appearance and character.

Top: With the tender well-stacked with coal, the pioneer 'B17,' *Sandringham* herself, stands at the water column at Cambridge shed in 1956. No. 61600 had a life of exactly 30 years, being built in 1928 and withdrawn in 1958. In the background, smoke from the substantial seven-road shed drifts up through the vents.

Above: At the north end of Cambridge, 'B12' 4-6-0 No. 61533 marshals a freight train for March, during November 1959. These inside-cylinder 4-6-0s had a distinctive air - and certainly looked better in photographs when 'caught' with the 'rods down.'

STEPHEN CROOK'S CLASSIC STEAM COLLECTION

Left: The return working of the Cambridge-Mildenhall goods approaches the main line at Barnwell Junction, about two miles north of Cambridge Station. The engine is 'J17' 0-6-0 No 65520, a GER Holden design of 1901. Although within the Cambridge City limits, the branch line atmosphere is heightened by the allotments in the foreground, with a fine display of rhubarb on the right. The date is May 1960.

Below: Passing Fulbourne, with a Newmarket-Cambridge local goods train in October 1959, is 'B12' 4-6-0 No. 61530, a few weeks before the engine was withdrawn. Taken out of service in November 1959, No. 61530 was scrapped within the month at Stratford Works. The leading wagon appears to be a single load of sugar beet, formerly a source of considerable rail freight traffic in East Anglia.

Above: The 1.55pm through train from Cambridge to Birmingham approaching Histon in October 1959, behind 'D16/3' 4-4-0 No. 62618. This engine (a former royal duties locomotive which was kept especially clean) would probably be detached at Peterborough. Not surprisingly, the train usually consisted principally of LMS stock. Passengers making the whole journey must have wondered whether they would not have done better to have paid more and gone via London; the cross-country journey took 5hr 10min to complete the 140 mile trip. This entailed visiting both stations at Peterborough - and at Peterborough North there was a pause of about half-an-hour.

Above: The Cambridge line was an obvious diversionary route when there was permanent way work on the GNR main line. On a May Sunday evening in 1960, 'A3' class 'Pacific' No 60055 *Woolwinder* (in very clean condition) passes Trumpington signalbox with a Down express. The engine is carrying an inverted headboard on the bufferbeam. No. 60055 was one of only four 'A3s' that late in 1959 were fitted with small wing-type smoke deflectors, alongside the chimney. Unfortunately they were not very successful, otherwise the 'A3s' would probably have been spared the hideous (in my view!) German-type deflectors later inflicted on most of the class. No. 60055 was withdrawn early - in September 1961 – and was thus the only one of the class to be scrapped in the condition in which she is seen here.

STEPHEN CROOK'S CLASSIC STEAM COLLECTION

THE LONDON AREA

Above: Country railways in Buckinghamshire: the push-pull train to Chalfont & Latimer leaves from the terminus at Chesham with a mid-day train in June 1958. The antique coaches are former Metropolitan Railway converted electric stock. The engine is a Robinson 'C13' class 4-4-2T, No 67418. This locomotive survived only until December 1958.

Left: The pride of Kingmoor: pioneer LMS 'Pacific' No 46200 *The Princess Royal* looks a treat in immaculate maroon livery, on shed at Camden in June 1962. No. 46200 slipped through the preservation net: following withdrawal in November 1962, the locomotive was stored at Carlisle until September 1964. It was then transferred to Connell's yard at Coatbridge and scrapped in October of that year. The engine behind is 'Royal Scot' 4-6-0 No. 46157, whilst English Electric Type 4 (later Class 40) No. D210 *Empress of Britain* is in the background.

STEPHEN CROOK'S CLASSIC STEAM COLLECTION

Facing page: Main line railways in London: Stanier 'Princess Royal' class 'Pacific' No. 46209 *Princess Beatrice* confidently climbs the bank through Camden in April 1962, with the 4.30pm train to Northampton and Rugby. Certainly, we were very fortunate to have some of the 'Princess Royals' working again at this time, after their 'hibernation' in store.

Above: Rebuilt 'Patriot' 4-6-0 No. 45525 *Colwyn Bay* stands at the arrival platforms of the old Euston terminus, in 1952. This shot was taken because I wanted a picture of a rebuilt 'Patriot' or 'Royal Scot' without the (then) new smoke deflectors, particularly as I thought they looked better without them. This indeed proved to be the last time that I saw an 'unblinkered' class 7P. This photograph was taken using a time exposure – with my camera 'propped up' on the buffer stops. Note the small LNWR 'ground dolly' alongside the rear driving wheel. How Euston has changed!

Left: One of the last 'Royal Scot' class 4-6-0s to remain in its original condition was No. 46156 *The South Wales Borderer*, seen at Willesden shed in 1953. It was rebuilt with a taper boiler the following year, and withdrawn ten years later in October 1964. The GWR 'Castle' of the same name was embellished with the regimental badge, whereas No. 46156 was one of the few 'Royal Scots' not to be thus favoured.

Right: A clean 'N2' 0-6-2T, No. 69568, climbs Holloway Bank, from King's Cross, in March 1964 with a transfer freight. This goods line seems to have a tunnel mouth and bore of its own. The pipes on either side of the engine's boiler were part of the condensing apparatus fitted for working through the London tunnels. Note the tiny lean-to against the wall on the cutting side on the right: was this the lair of a regular spotter?! The neatly pruned shrubs between the tracks were a well-known feature on Holloway bank.

Below: A classic London suburban scene, now the preserve of rather characterless electric multiple units. A Palace Gates-North Woolwich train leaves Stratford Low Level in September 1961, against a typical east end background of crumbling warehouses. The engine, No. 69640, is a class N7/3, indicating it has been rebuilt with a round-topped boiler, but retaining short-travel valves.

STEPHEN CROOK'S CLASSIC STEAM COLLECTION

Left: No doubt suffering withdrawal symptoms, the disembodied smokebox of a 'J69' 0-6-0T looks appropriately forlorn as it waits to be taken away from Stratford in 1952.

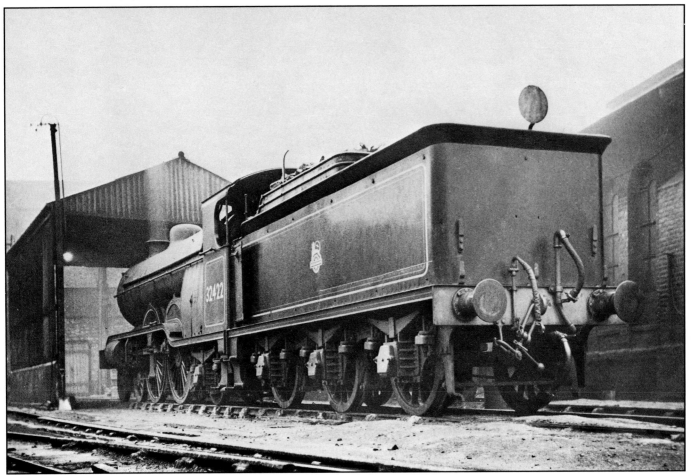

Above: Handsome from any angle, Brighton 'Atlantic' No. 32422 *North Foreland* stands by the inspection pit at Stewart's Lane shed, on a winter's afternoon in 1952. Designed by Marsh and built in 1911, 32422 was withdrawn in 1956. These were the last 4-4-2 tender engines to survive in Britain. Stewarts Lane shed, at Battersea, was the depot for Victoria.

THE SOUTHERN REGION

Right: 'U1' class 2-6-0 No. 31908 steams past west of Woking, in October 1962, with a down Basingstoke train. The 'U1s' were very similar in appearance to the more numerous 'N' class, the principal difference being that the former had 6ft driving wheels (compared with the 'N's' 5ft 6in) which thereby required small splashers. The postwar *ABC of Southern Locomotives* tells us that these engines were nicknamed 'U boats', a term that would easily spring to mind at that time.

Below: The last surviving 'N15' class 'King Arthur' 4-6-0 of the original series, No 30451 *Sir Lamorak* leaves Brookwood with a down afternoon Basingstoke train, in October 1961. This engine was finally withdrawn in June 1962. The shape of the cab roof was the principal visible difference between these 'Eastleigh Arthurs' and the later engines. The fine LSWR lower quadrant signals guarding the exit to the station have already returned to the 'on' position. I remember Brookwood as the station where our school corps detrained for the annual camp. The best thing about Pirbright Camp was that you could look down on the main line without actually leaving the premises!

STEPHEN CROOK'S CLASSIC STEAM COLLECTION

Above: 'Lord Nelson' 4-6-0 No 30857 *Lord Howe* hurries up to town with a local train from Basingstoke, in October 1961. I had actually intended to photograph the train in the cutting beyond the bridge, but the sun was only just starting to penetrate it. The location is near Farnborough.

Above: 'Schools' class 4-4-0 No 30902 *Wellington* near Hook with the 1.54pm Waterloo-Basingstoke in October 1961. Introduced by Maunsell in 1930 at a time when this wheel arrangement was becoming unfashionable, the 'Schools' neverthless proved to be one of the most successful 4-4-0s ever built. They were also the most powerful 4-4-0s in Britain. Exactly half the class were fitted with multiple jet blast-pipes and a large diameter chimney, which somewhat detracted from their appearance. No. 30902 fortunately is in original condition. By this time the 'Schools' were seeing their last months active service. The white route disc in the '3 o'clock' position indicated a Basingstoke 'stopping' train.

Right: Of the larger SR engines that survived until the 1960s, the Class N15X 'Remembrance' 4-6-0s must have been amongst the most handsome. When I took this picture of No. 32331 *Beattie* at Basingstoke, late in 1956, it was the only survivor of a small class of just seven engines. These had been rebuilt from Class L 4-6-4T tank engines in the 1930s. I remember that although I was an unofficial visitor, the foreman insisted on having the engine towed out of the shed for me - the sort of incident it is particularly pleasing to record and recall.

Left: The Dunton Green-Westerham branch train hurries past near Brasted Halt, just a week before the closure of the line on October 28 1961. No. 31324 is one of Wainwright's class H 0-4-4Ts built for the SECR. This branch, of almost five miles, was near Sevenoaks.

Below: Of the smaller SR engines that survived until the mid-1960s, the 'Q1' class 0-6-0s must have been the least handsome! At least their unfinished appearance could be attributed to their emergence in 1942, in the middle of the war. The 'SR ABC' records their popular name as 'Charlies'. Here, No. 33036 (of Guildford shed) is heading west through Woking woods in July 1963. At least the dullness of the wagons is in keeping with the lines of the locomotive.

Above: 'Lord Nelson' 4-6-0 No 30862 *Lord Collingwood* west of Basingstoke in October 1961 with a down Southampton train. The 'Lord Nelsons' were mainly confined to the Waterloo-Southampton main line and although there were only 16 examples, they always seemed more numerous.

Above: The only railway still open on the Isle of Wight in 1966 linked Ryde and Ventnor. All trains were worked by Adams '02' class 0-4-4Ts built between 1889 and 1895. One of the major attractions was the continued use of vintage coaching stock of a type which had long since disappeared from the mainland. No doubt this was partly due to the diffi- culty of transferring stock 'over the water'. No 27 *Merstone* is seen near Brading with an early morning train from Ryde to Ventnor. All the engines were named after towns or villages on the island - some travellers, I hear, confused the locomotive names of this type with destination boards!

STEPHEN CROOK'S CLASSIC STEAM COLLECTION

'A1X' class 'Terrier' 0-6-0T No. 32646 heads for Hayling Island in July 1961. It is approaching Langstone Station, just north of Langstone Bridge, which connected the island to the mainland. It was because of this wooden bridge that these lightweight engines had to be used. It was also because of this wooden bridge that all the engines had to be fitted with spark arresters – yet even with a spark arrester fitted, the top of the chimney is lower than the top of the coaches! The branch was closed in November 1963, chiefly because of the advancing decay of the harbour bridge.

Right: The lightly-laid and tortuous curvature of the Axminster-Lyme Regis branch fortunately led to the retention of three of these splendid engines. Adams 4-4-2 radial tank No. 30583 leaves Axminster in October 1960, with an afternoon train to Lyme Regis. However, LMS Ivatt 2-6-2Ts were allowed to take over in 1961. The branch closed in November 1965, but this engine survives on the Bluebell Railway.

Below: The best time to visit the Lyme Regis branch was a summer Saturday, when the 10.45am train from Waterloo included through coaches to Lyme Regis, requiring the use of two engines down the branch. Here, the 10.45am is seen between Axminster and Combpyne on June 18 1960, with the numerically neat combination of 30583 and 30584 in charge. The most apparent difference between the two engines is in the shape of the frame ends visible below the smokebox - with 30583 retaining the original design. With either style there was a slight recess between the frame ends and the buffer-beam, making it a convenient place for carrying spare lamps or oil cans, and 30583 seems to be making full use of this space. There certainly was not much spare room anywhere else on these engines. Another point of difference between the two is that 30583 has a larger dome. No. 30584 was withdrawn in January 1961, and scrapped, whilst 30583 was taken out of service in July 1961, for preservation.

Below: An evening train leaves Exeter Central for Exmouth in June 1960. The pilot is an LMS Ivatt 2-6-2T No. 41318, whilst the train engine is the rather more powerful '3MT' 'Standard' 2-6-2T No. 82018.

Left: Beattie 2-4-0 well tank No. 30587 at work on the Wadebridge to Wenfordbridge branch in north Cornwall, in June 1960. This was another line where weight restrictions and sharp curves had forced the retention of older motive power. It was primarily a freight line to deal with the clay traffic from Wenfordbridge. Here, the train is halted before the crossing with the main road near Dunmere. The train has just entered the actual Wenfordbridge line at Dunmere Junction, which involved unlocking a gate across the track. The driver is waiting for the guard to return the keys to the box at Boscarne Junction (one third of a mile back from Dunmere Junction) where the line to Bodmin North diverges from the line to Bodmin General. After 87 years of service (incredibly surviving the rest of the class by more than 60 years), the three remaining well tanks finally ceased operating in August 1962. They were replaced by WR '1366' class 0-6-0 pannier tanks.

The driver is seen as a silhouette in the cab spectacle as 'T9' 4-4-0 No. 30313 runs besides the Camel estuary with a mid-day train from Wadebridge to Padstow, in June 1960. This five and a half mile branch was very under-used, with no intermediate stations. With its wide cab and splashers and small six-wheeled tender, this variety of T9 looks appreciably different from No. 30120 (see page 3) Introduced in 1899, the 'T9s' had a very long life, and were still working passenger trains in the 1960s; they certainly earned their keep.

THE WESTERN REGION

Above: Roundhouses always generated a very special atmosphere and the expression 'cathedrals of steam' is very apt. The front end of GWR 'King' 4-6-0 No 6014 *King Henry VII* is seen inside Old Oak Common shed, in 1953. For those of you looking at this in black and white (!) the engine is painted in blue livery! When this picture was taken, most of the 'Kings' had already returned to Brunswick green. Anyway, I am glad I took this, as it is the only picture I have of a 'King' with the lovely original chimney. At a large shed like this, which consisted of several 'roundhouses' under one roof, the individual smoke vents were certainly a very necessary feature.

Below: GWR veteran: 'Star' class 4-6-0 No. 4056 *Princess Margaret* stands in the yard at Old Oak Common, in 1953. The cab looks rather primitive. This engine has the elbow-shaped steam pipes that appeared on some of the class after the fitting of new inside cylinders. They looked rather awkward from the front, although acceptable from this angle. This engine survived until October 1957, and was the last of the class to be withdrawn. It is interesting to recall that in those days Old Oak Common shed, despite its size and importance, was a completely open site, without even a token fence to discourage unofficial visitors - thank goodness!

Right: The nameplate of 'Star' 4-6-0 No 4056. The lack of beading on the top of the splasher immediately distinguishes it from the more modern GWR classes. The GWR was not keen on long names otherwise they might have included the 'Rose', certainly none of the 'Star' nameplates had two lines.

STEPHEN CROOK'S CLASSIC STEAM COLLECTION

Collett 2-6-2T No. 6135 hurries through Sonning Cutting with an up parcels train in July 1963.

Right: 'Castle' class 4-6-0 No 5020 *Trematon Castle* approaches the western end of Sonning Cutting, in July 1963, with the 1.55pm Paddington-Swansea train. The prefix 'F' on the reporting number indicated a South Wales destination. The flat-sided tenders, as paired here with No. 5020, were originally fitted to the newer BR-built 'Castles' in the 7000 series, but inevitably they soon appeared with older engines. Despite the idyllic appearance of the surroundings, this was the only lineside spot in Britain where I encountered a snake in the grass.........fortunately, it was the first to beat a retreat!

Below: After a brief signal check, 2-8-0 No. 4707 gets on the move again at Reading with a down freight, in July 1963. These 2-8-0s, Churchward's last design, were successful on both freight and passenger workings, and it is a pity that only nine examples were built. The GWR, alone of the 'Big Four' companies, remained faithful to lower quadrant signals, rather than introducing the upper quadrant variety as a safer device.

Left: The last rites for the 'Kings' were on the London-Wolverhampton trains, and they were the regular motive power for all expresses until the end of 1962. In May of that year, No 6012 *King Edward VI* is approaching the Chiltern summit at Saunderton, with a down Wolverhampton express. No. 6012 was taken out of service less than four months later: scrapping followed in October 1963 at Oldbury, in the West Midlands.

Above: Hatton Bank, near Warwick, presented westbound trains with a three-miles climb at about 1 in 110. Here, 'Castle' class 4-6-0 No 4096 *Highclere Castle* is tackling the ascent on September 29 1962, with a through train from Margate to Wolverhampton. In the circumstances the combination of Western motive power and mixed Mk1/Southern stock seems appropriate. No. 4096 is carrying an 81C shedplate, and the excellent external condition of the engine, with the running plate and frames as clean as the boiler, is a tribute to the cleaners at Southall shed. The jet of water over the tender indicates that the fireman is hosing down the coal to settle the dust.

THE WESTERN REGION

Above: 'Hall' class 4-6-0 No 6913 *Levens Hall* climbs Hatton Bank with a down passenger train on September 29 1962. Levens Hall was actually out of the GWR area, in Westmorland, but the GWR had inevitably been forced to cast its net fairly wide to find enough names for this large class. This is another commendably clean engine, this time from Reading shed (81D). The impression is given that quite a high number of cleaners on the Western region must have been laid off at the end of 1962, judging by deteriorating locomotive cleanliness thereafter.

Above: Descending Hatton Bank with a ballast train on September 29 1962 is Churchward '4300' class 'Mogul' No. 6394. This was one of those rare days when every engine which passed seemed to be clean. This Gloucester engine appears to be not long out of the works. At this time, No. 6394 had less than two years life remaining: withdrawn in June 1964, the 2-6-0 was demolished for scrap by the end of the year.

Left: '7400' class 0-6-0PT No. 7424 makes haste on the lower reaches of Hatton Bank, apparently in charge of a lightweight down engineers train in July 1963.

Left: Splendidly antiquated in appearance, 'Dukedog' 4-4-0 No. 9017 waits to leave Pwllheli with the 4.5pm to Machynlleth, in June 1960. These engines were a marvellous exception to the possible criticism, from some linesiders' point of view, that most GWR classes tended to look rather similar! Although the building date was officially 1936, they were in fact a happy hybrid of some of Dean's much earlier 'Duke' and 'Bulldog' engines from the last century, a union reflected in the name. By fitting a 'Duke' boiler onto 'Bulldog' frames an engine was produced which was light enough for the Cambrian lines. By October 1960, No. 9017 had been withdrawn, and was sent to Oswestry prior to preservation on the Bluebell Railway. Unfortunately this is my only picture from Wales, but at least it is well and truly in Wales, not just over the border!

Right: The 'Kings' lived up to their name: they were certainly majestic: No. 6018 *King Henry VI* is seen alongside the coaling stage at Swindon in April 1963, in connection with one of the 'last King runs'. Somebody has made an excellent job of painting the number on the bufferbeam, and with the smokebox door numberplate removed, the engine is half-way towards being in GWR condition. Unfortunately nothing could be done abut the chimney; I felt they always looked better with the original design. With the continuous use of soft Welsh steam coal, the GWR never implemented mechanised coaling, which would have reduced the fuel to dust. GWR sheds relied principally on muscle power, small tipping tubs and gravity to replenish tenders and bunkers.

Facing page: The GWR branches undeniably had a unique atmosphere and appeal. This is '45XX' class 2-6-2T No. 5553, climbing from Bodmin Road station to Bodmin General with the 4.25pm to Wadebridge and Padstow in May 1961. These later engines of the '45XX' class had larger tanks, which gave them a rather less neat appearance, in my view. This service did not operate on Sundays. If we include Bodmin Road, the small, if important town of Bodmin boasted three stations at this time. Bodmin Road was on the Plymouth-Truro main line, around three and a half miles from Bodmin General.

THE SOMERSET & DORSET LINE

Right: The first of Fowler's '7F' 2-8-0s built for the SDJR, No 53800, stands outside Bath shed in August 1951. It is interesting to recall that the shed code for Bath at that time was 71G, indicating that it was then a sub-shed of Eastleigh. The primitive illumination, the fine selection of fire irons leaning against the wall, and the shortage of planks in the front of the shed building all contribute towards a typical shed scene of the times.

Below: The last SDJR 2-8-0, No 53810, passes Wellow with a southbound train on a September Saturday in 1961. Classified '7F', these engines were quite often seen on passenger trains at busy times and they gave the line much of its unique character.

As well known a location as any on the 'S&D' was this view at Midford, with the southbound 'Pines Express' drifting down over the viaduct before attacking the climb to Wellow, in September 1961. At the time, I was very disappointed not to see a '2P' 4-4-0 as pilot engine, especially as they had only just been displaced from most pilot duties. At any rate we have a typical S&D mixture on display: 'Standard' 4-6-0 No. 75023 in green livery, indicating Western Region affiliations, piloting SR unrebuilt 'West Country' light 'Pacific' No. 34041 *Wilton*. The train is a mixture of LMS and BR coaches, the fourth vehicle being a heavy LMS 12-wheeled restaurant car. Overlooking the train is a fine LSWR signal. This location had been less good in the 1950s, as there had been an awkward lineside hut on the nearside of the track opposite No. 75023. The following year, the 'Pines Express' was re-routed via Oxford, a step which marked the beginning of the end for the 'S&D.' The line finally closed on March 7 1966.

Below: Fowler 'S&D' 7F 2-8-0 No. 53808, probably not long out of the workshops, prepares to leave Midsomer Norton with a northbound freight in May 1962. The gradient post just in front of the engine indicates an easy trip for the short distance to Radstock, most of it downhill at 1 in 50. The fireman may be able to sit down for a few minutes with a 'lid' of tea from his billycan.

Right: '3F' 0-6-0 No. 43216 leaves Wincanton in May 1962, with a 'local' from Highbridge to Templecombe, despite the apparently erroneous headcode. The normal 'S&D' headcode for passenger trains (express or local) was one lamp in front of the chimney and one over the left buffer. These Johnson engines of 1896 were built specifically for the SDJR. By this time, their 'S&D' days were nearly over and the GWR '2251' 0-6-0s were handling some of these trains.

Rear cover, upper: The Gloucester-Chalford 'auto' climbs away from Stroud with an afternoon train in October 1964, in the charge of Collett 0-4-2T No. 1444, which had been withdrawn by the end of the month. By December, the service itself had gone too.

Rear cover, lower: 'V2' 2-6-2 No. 60937 pounds the last mile to Whitrope summit on April 8 1961 with the 11.15am Carlisle-Millerhill freight. In the early 1960s, after the withdrawal of the 'K3s', nearly all Waverley freights were hauled by 'V2s.'

STEPHEN CROOK'S CLASSIC STEAM COLLECTION